Love is not enough

Love is not enough

Rachel Schmidt

TARGUM/FELDHEIM

First published 2000
Copyright © 2000 by Rachel Schmidt
ISBN 1-56871-157-3

Published by:
Targum Press, Inc.
22700 W. Eleven Mile Rd.
Southfield, MI 48034
E-mail: targum@elronet.co.il
Fax toll free: (888) 298-9992

Distributed by:
Feldheim Publishers
200 Airport Executive Park
Nanuet, NY 10954
www.feldheim.com

Printed in Israel

LOVE IS NOT ENOUGH

"An eye-opener for educators and parents alike, Mrs. Schmidt provides information and guidance with real-life situations along with a dose of always useful chizuk."

Mrs. R. Malinowitz, MA
Principal, Deal Yeshiva-Bet Yaakov

"Rachel Schmidt offers penetrating insights and great advice...a must for the Jewish home."

Rebbetzin Vella Horowitz
Bostoner Rebbetzin

"Finally, a book that stands up to the challenges of raising healthy, erlech children in a world of confusion."

Rebbetzin Esther Steinwurzel
Congregation Bais Ephraim

"To every parent who struggles with child-rearing, Rachel Schmidt's book is a welcome oasis in the desert of confusion. Highly recommended for every home and every high-school class."

Chaya Sara Stark, MA
Educational Evaluator, B.Y. Seminary Educator of
Teaching Methods

"Enchanting, educational, and inspirational reading that cannot be put down. A must for every Jewish mother."

Shani Fasten née Hecht
Daughter of Rabbi Abraham B. Hecht

"This is a wonderful resource for all teachers of domestic science and human development. No Jewish young adult should graduate without reading this vital book on the basic principles of child development and proper Jewish parenting...a must-have for every high school and seminary."

Miriam Ungar, MA, MED
Educational Consultant

"This educational book is so fascinatingly interesting, it is hard to put it down. For reference, entertainment, and guidance, this remarkably educational experience leaves emotional impressions to last a lifetime! Parenting will never be the same after reading this book."

Esther Huttner
Early Childhood Educator
Daughter of Reb Mendel Kaplan from Philadelphia

"Love Is Not Enough must be addressed in every high school class and Jewish home. Healthy parenting is not inborn... It is a skill that has to be learned again and again."

Miriam Amsel, CSW
Mechaneches in Machon Bais Yaakov High School
Social Worker at ODA of Williamsburg

"In the midst of today's secularism, Rachel Schmidt's book brings warmth and Yiddishkeit into the Jewish home."

Rebbetzin Chavie Paneth
Congregation Deiszh

In memory
of those very special people whose love
and dedication in
"Raising Emotionally Healthy Yiddishe Children"
have been the backbone behind
the parenting classes,
learning center for parents, and this book.

לזכר נשמת

ר׳ מנחם מנדל בן יחיא-ל מיכל
שרה בת אלטר ישעיה
בריינדל בת יהושע
ר׳ יעקב בן אברהם יצחק
ר׳ ישרא-ל מענדל בן אברהם

CONTENTS

About the Author

The author writes about her life:
I was born in Hungary in 1952, in the house where my mother had been born. In 1956, during the Hungarian revolution, my family was given sudden permission to leave the country but was barred by quotas from entering the United States. Stranded in Vienna for two years, I began my education in an antisemitic public school where I was harassed daily for being an Orthodox Jew.

We finally arrived in New York in 1959, and I was immediately placed in Bais Yaakov. While my older sisters caught on to the Hebrew, Yiddish, and English subjects with ease, I trailed far behind. A poor student in all subjects, I was stigmatized as "lazy" and "dumb."

During my last year in school, one teacher paid close attention to me and convinced me that I was just as smart as everyone else in the class. It took a lot of effort, cajoling, and consistent encouragement to convince me, but my teacher did not give up. She instilled confidence in me by asking me to substitute for the class during her absence and reading my poetry and stories to the class. By the time graduation arrived, much to everyone's surprise, I had passed all the Regents and received a state-certified diploma.

The confidence instilled by that one lone teacher bore many fruits. During the next three years, I launched the first homebound program and Meals on Wheels to shut-ins for Agudath Israel, volunteered at Chronic Disease Hospital, and tutored disturbed children at Ohel Children's Home, all while teaching preschool. In 1973 the Human Resources Department awarded me Volunteer of the Year due to my Agudah project, bringing great publicity and a *kiddush Hashem* nationwide.

It took another twenty years for me to return to school so that I could begin a career in social work. The fear of failure was so deeply rooted that my husband came to class with me; I felt I could not do it on my own. When I graduated Wurzweiler School of Social Work at Yeshiva University in 1991, I had scored the highest in my class and came in third among the entire graduating class.

After graduation, I launched a successful social service department at ODA Primary Center in Williamsburg, Brooklyn. I also began giving parenting classes, was the first Orthodox social worker to be invited to join the committee of Prevention of Child Abuse at Beth Israel Hospital, implemented play therapy as a means of reaching Orthodox children who cannot express themselves with words, and worked to dispel the stigma of therapy from the Orthodox community. At the same time, I taught *hashkafah* to eleventh-graders at Machon Bais Yaakov, was guidance counselor for Bais Yaakov of Boro Park, and a member of the board of directors at Maimonides Mental Health Center.

Today I have two practices: The Learning Center, which deals only with children, and a separate private practice for adults.

During my free time I thrive on spoiling my grandchildren, spending time doing "nothing special" with my children, and writing in the wee hours of the night. My greatest accomplishment? Being an *eizer kenegdo* (helpmate) to my husband, both when he was a *kollel* student and through his career as acting supreme judge in the Civil Court, and raising my children to be healthy, *frum* individuals, similar and yet different one from the other.

Many Thanks...

With tremendous gratitude to Hashem for giving me the *zechus* to be a messenger for both children and adults, I feel humbled and inspired at the same time. I am fortunate to have had a diversified repertoire of friends, *mechanchim*, colleagues, and professionals who have encouraged me to implement practical means of meeting the psychological and spiritual needs of the developing child.

None of this would have been possible without the *berachos* of so many *gedolim* of the past and present, who have given me their blessings both professionally and personally: the Satmar Rebbe, Rabbi Yoel Teitelbaum, *zt"l*; the Gerrer Rebbes; the Lubavitcher Rebbe, Rabbi Menachem Mendel Schneerson; Rav Schach of Ponevezh; the Ribnitzer Rebbe, *zt"l*; the Skulener Rebbe, Rabbi Yaakov Stefansky; and Reb Hershele of Spinka, *zt"l*. I am convinced that without their prayers, this book would never have gotten off the ground.

Perhaps no one deserves more credit than Rabbi Joshua Silbermintz, *z"l*, former president of Pirchei Agudath Israel, for being the first to recognize my potential. When I was a challenging eighteen-year-old, he urged me to channel my energies into becoming involved in a productive project. And so we started NAJR, which turned into Project SEED and later Meals on Wheels to meet the emotional and physical needs of the elderly homebound and those in institutions. The pioneer project turned into a national haven for the hundreds of adopted grandmothers visited on a weekly basis. Rabbi Silbermintz's message that one can make the impossible happen if he works hand in hand with *hishtadlus* and *siyatta diShamaya* still rings in my ears thirty years later when I need the motivation to go on.

My sincerest appreciation to Rabbi Oscar Ehrenreich of Bais Yaakov of Boro Park for his decades of belief in me during my elementary years as a student, and later as a PRE-1A teacher, and more recently as a guidance counselor and now as a clinical social worker.

I feel privileged to have received Rabbi Laibel Katz's enthusiastic response to the parenting seminars for improving Jewish education both at home and in the classroom.

I want to extend my appreciation to Rabbi Tzvi Kestenbaum, director of ODA Medical Center in Williamsburg, for placing such confidence and trust in me; Dr. Robert Kraus, clinical director of ODA Medical Center, for instilling within me the ideas and support to begin such a worthy project; and executive secretary Chayele Zilberberg, for editing and typing this book.

More than any other experience, being the *hashkafah* teacher in Machon Bais Yaakov has taught me to appreciate and understand the needs of teenagers. When students are privileged to have a *menahel* like Rabbi Yehuda Oelbaum, who exemplifies *ahavas Yisrael* and personal devotion to *klal Yisrael*, it is no surprise that they become shining examples of a true *bas Yisrael*.

Perhaps no educator has had such a strong impact on my

hashkafos as Rabbi Moshe Faigelstock, *rosh yeshivah* of Tiferes Elimelech. To thank him for being a principal, *mechanech*, and devoted father figure, not only to his students but to his teachers as well, seems inadequate. The most honorable way to show gratitude is to spread his standard of education to others. This book is in large part based on the lessons he has personally role-modeled for me.

A special thanks to my teacher, mentor, and role model, Sara Freund, CSW. Like a mother to her child, you have coached my initial dream of becoming a social worker by walking me through the six years it took to become one. Today, as directors at the Learning Center for Parents, we have created probably the first professional forum where the emotional needs of children are of the utmost importance and children can be attended to discreetly in a private setting rather than a government-funded agency.

Only Hashem can repay Rebbetzin Miriam Amsel, *mechaneches* of Machon Bais Yaakov High School and social worker at ODA, for standing by twenty-four hours a day as an ethical consultant; Devorah Heller for her encouragement in seeing the silver lining behind every cloud; Rachel Deutch, Rebbetzins Ruth Shaingarten and Matti Shaingarten, and Rifka Rabinowitz, CSW, for believing that I could overcome the spiritual and educational tribulations of returning to school despite the fact that I was never a good student. Their fierce trust and confidence turned my lifelong dream into a reality.

Thank you Country Yossi for making my articles famous by publishing them in your magazine; Mrs. Yenty Rosenfeld for being a loyal secretary and having the capacity to do ten things at one time; Shaindle Kanstam for her expertise in computers; Chavi Schmidt, my daughter-in-law, for submitting my children's stories into the international *Hamodia* newspaper; Yidu Zellermeir, my son-in-law, for being my technical support and graphic artist; and Chaya Sarah Stark and Miriam Unger for painfully plowing through my manuscript page by page.

Sara, Dvorah, Toby, Gitty, and Miriam, my sisters, we struggled together as young immigrants, not knowing a word of English, to become successful mothers, raising beautiful families. With a mere ten dollars tuition for all of us, Bais Yaakov of Williamsburg patched our wings of migrant fear until we had the courage to fly and soar high. Many years later, as alumni of Bais Yaakov Teacher's Seminary, we are eternally indebted to our mentors, not merely for teaching us the text of the Torah, but for imbuing us with love and appreciation of being a *bas Yisrael*. I hope that this book will be just one source of pride and *nachas* to them. Joining forces with them once again in molding my daughter Sara Breindel, who is in tenth grade, to become one of the next generation of *Yiddishe mamas* is the highest pinnacle of trust I can bestow upon the former and present teachers and principals, Rebbetzin Kaplan, *a"h*, Rebbetzin Kirzner, Rebbetzin Goldhirsh, and Rabbi Hellman.

Words cannot express my gratitude to my parents, Mr. and Mrs. Klein, for the sacrifices they have made for providing me with the highest caliber of Jewish education; my children, Srulie, Zissy, Yoel, and Sara Breindel for bearing with my mistakes in parenting; my precious grandchildren, Saraleh and Zissel Aidel, for making my life sweeter than candy; and my husband, Judge Schmidt, for his unconditional support throughout the years.

May *HaKadosh Baruch Hu* grant me the privilege of continuing to bring *nachas* and comfort to all who seek my expertise.

Introduction

A MOTHER of eight healthy children approached her rabbi with tears streaming down her face. Her distress was so acute that the rabbi gently urged her, "Tell me, what can I do for you? What troubles you?"

The woman looked down as she choked on the words that struggled to emerge. "I have a wonderful family. They would be a joy to any Jewish parent — until one day, out of the blue, my Binyamin ran away from home. It took us two weeks to locate him in a hostel in Manhattan. He refused to come home. He said he never wants to be *frum* again."

The woman couldn't go on. She buried her head in her hands and sobbed convulsively. "What did I do wrong?" she lamented. "I was equally devoted to all my eight children. I fed them all the same, I taught them the prayers all the same, and I disciplined them all the same..."

"I'm sorry," interrupted the rabbi, "but that was your mistake — you treated them all the same."

The lesson of this story can break every mother's heart. Don't we all try to be good parents to our children? Don't we dedicate and even sacrifice our lives for our children so that they, too, will continue the tradition of *Yiddishkeit* we so conscientiously instill in them daily almost all of our waking hours? How, then, could the woman in the story find herself in such a tragic situation?

Each child is a world unto himself. While the primary needs of all children are the same, not every child requires the same approach to discipline nor the same expressions of love and affection. One five-year-old child may be content with a smile or a pat on the head; another may need a lot of affectionate hugs to feel as loved. To one ten-year-old child, discipline in the form of a stern look is enough to remind him that his actions are inappropriate, while to another, even a verbal reminder is not enough. One newborn may be content to simply be fed and changed before he is able to return to a blissful sleep. Another infant may fuss for hours, demanding physical soothing before falling into a restful sleep.

Can we mothers be versatile? Can we be flexible in the way we nurture? Can we adapt to the temperament and personality of the child? The more educated the mother is in how to meet the emotional needs of each of her children, the more likely the fruits of her labor will yield bushels of *nachas*.

TWO LADIES were sitting together at a wedding making small talk. "How many children do you have?"

"One," replied the other.

"One? How can that be? I heard you have two married children and just had a baby five months ago."

The mother smiled. "I really do have only one — one of each kind."

Mother's Needs versus the Child's Needs

Being prepared to meet the individual emotional needs of every child is not enough — one must know how to meet those needs appropriately. Experts on child development say that loving a child is not enough. One must question one's own motives in the way one expresses love. Is the experience of mothering fulfilling your own personal needs, or is it meeting the needs of the child?

When a child claims to have eaten enough for supper, and we pressure the child to eat just one more spoonful and then still another spoonful, we need to stop and question our motives. Are we being driven by our need to "show off" a plump, red-cheeked baby to display our competence as mothers, basking each time someone comments on her cute, round face? When we insist on putting several layers of clothes on the child who claims to be hot, are we trying to meet his need to be warm or our need to protect the child? The mother who attends to her child all day, fussing over his schedule nonstop, disregarding all other interests in life, running to pick him up at the first whimper, may be responding, not to the needs of the child, but to her internal anxieties about being a good mother.

Staying attuned to our needs versus the needs of the child is vital in raising emotionally healthy children. Too often, being unaware of our insecurities, we unconsciously manipulate the situation into a source of gratification for ourselves rather than for the child.

The Way We Parent Reflects the Parenting We Received

Some mothers seem to have a natural flair for parenting, while others grope in the dark, never knowing for sure if they are doing the right thing. What determines the competence of a mother? Why would a mother of two be a nervous wreck at the end of the day, while a mother of ten may find the patience to give each child a good-night hug and kiss?

The answer lies both in the temperament of the mother and the quality of parenting she received as a child. If she was raised in an emotionally healthy environment where love flowed freely and easily when she was an infant and later replaced with both love and discipline, she will naturally raise her family the same way. She will find herself using the same methods of parenting her own parents used because they have been ingrained in her.

If, however, the family environment was unable to provide the mother with unconditional love, affection, and attention when she was a child, she will find it difficult to provide these essential foundations to her children. Before a child can learn to give, love, share, and nurture others, he must be given to and nurtured unconditionally as an infant. Later, there has to be a blend of love and discipline to provide guidance, self-control, and healthy maturation.

Of course, we know that everyone has free will; we can change through working on our *middos*. No one should feel she has no hope of overcoming a difficult background. For ourselves, we must not use any lacks in our own childhood as an excuse.

At the same time, we do our utmost to give our children all they need to make them, in turn, fine, caring parents. The future competency of our children depends to a large extent on the quality of parenting they are receiving today. Children are not born with the innate ability to nurture themselves and extend love to others; they depend on us, their parents, to teach it to them.

Why Do I Need This Book?

Many conscientious mothers ask, "Why the need for parenting books? Our parents and grandparents raised beautiful families successfully without books or seminars. I know all there is to know about parenting from my mother."

There is no doubt that we want to emulate the Jewish values of our parents. However, the challenges involved in raising children to follow in the footsteps of our grandparents have changed drastically. Here are a few examples:

1. In Europe, and even in postwar America, there were fewer conveniences like washing machines and dishwashers, so the physical aspect of parenting was more demanding. However, with luxuries such as dryers and microwaves came new, modern-day pressures our parents did not have. These include doing homework with three or four different students, all in different grades, both in English and Hebrew or Yiddish. As a matter of fact, most of our great-grandmothers didn't even go to school. Their education consisted of learning to read and write and watching their mothers kasher a chicken or prepare a live fish for Shabbos, canning preserves, and keeping kosher. Mothers of yesteryear did not have to practice davening with four-year-olds, review *Chumash* with five-year-olds, do science projects with eight-year-olds, and write compositions with ten-year-olds.

   In addition, teenagers were recruited to help with the housework. The teenagers of today usually can give little of their time to help their mothers because their overloaded schedules, full of tests, reports, midterms, finals, and Regents, with little time in between, do not allow for it. Knowing when to put your foot down and demand help and when to look the other way can become a major issue.

2. Another great difference is clothes. I lived in Hungary the first four years of my life. Dressing was simple then, efficient, no big hassle. We had a weekday dress with an apron, a Shabbos dress, and shoes to wear when it snowed. And we were considered well dressed.

   Today such a trousseau would be considered improper and negligent. Mothers today have to cope with decisions such as how many sets of clothes to buy their children without going overboard and spoiling them while at the same time preventing them from feeling like *nebs* compared to their friends.

3. As if we don't have enough decisions to make, we also have to deal with the matter of nosh. In Europe, this issue was nonexistent. In the summer, the nosh consisted of delicious fresh strawberries, and in the winter, if you got hold of oranges and apples you had a party. Cake was simple and baked for Shabbos or *simchahs*.

   Today our children consume so much nosh at home, friend's houses, parties, school canteens, after-school excursions to grocery stores for an "on the way home" snack, *simchahs*, Shabbos and *yom tov*, and from tender-loving *pekelech* from grandparents. If mothers don't take an active role in supervising their menu of sweets, not only will the children become sugar addicts and human bouncing candy machines, but they will probably spend much money and time at the dentist.

4. Today, not only do girls attend school, a relatively recent development, but toddlers do so as well. Children as young as two begin play group, soon to be followed by nursery school.

   Which grade should a bright three-year-old attend — play group, nursery, or kindergarten? Does the emotional level of the child coincide with his cognitive maturity? Making the wrong decision by putting a child in a class that does not fit his level of maturity can be detrimental to his long-term attitude toward school and learning in general.

And so, today's parents have issues to deal with that are vastly different from those our parents dealt with. To help them make the right decisions according to each child's needs, parenting books and seminars serve a vital purpose.

Birth to 2 Years

Trust versus Mistrust

Whether children come to trust or mistrust themselves and others largely depends on their early experience in life. If mother or caretaker meets the emotional needs of the infant through feeding, holding, and developing a genuine bond, the child will perceive the environment as safe and secure. His relationships in life are apt to be fulfilling and healthy.

In contrast, infants whose care is unpredictable and unloving tend to view the world as a threatening place. They may feel insecure about themselves as well as others. Their relationships in life are more likely to be unstable and nonproductive.

Training a baby by the book is a good idea, only you need a different book for each child.

— Dan Bennet

Three Basic Activities

There are three basic activities of all newborns: sleeping, crying, and eating. How parents respond to these activities plays a lifelong role in the emotional health of the child as he passes through the developmental stages of life and enters adulthood.

Sleeping

A newborn spends most of his time sleeping, so don't be alarmed if your baby sleeps much of the day and night. He is growing and developing while sleeping, so this is not an "empty" activity. Take advantage of these hours to catch up on much needed sleep or to give attention to the other siblings in the family.

Crying

While crying is a normal response of a newborn, it can be confusing and frustrating to the mother who is juggling an entire household. When parents cannot get their baby to stop crying, they sometimes wind up feeling distraught, helpless, angry at the baby, and guilty for experiencing this anger. If parents have difficulty getting their baby to stop crying, this does not mean they are neglectful or doing a bad job. Crying is a baby's chief way to communicate his need to be comforted, fed, changed, and held. Sometimes he is simply bored or fussy.

Many babies cry for a few minutes before settling down to sleep. If your baby fits this pattern, it is not wise to pick him up as soon as he starts crying. Give him time to fuss and fall asleep undisturbed.

— Two Views

Between 1920 and 1930, the United States Children's Bureau in Infant Care pamphlets advised mothers not to "give in" to the crying infant, since it would surely spoil the child. They felt that "a spoiled, fussy baby becomes a household tyrant whose continual demands make a slave of the mother."

Infant experts have altered their opinion a great deal. They now feel that a baby's cry isn't merely a sign of distress, but a powerful and basic tool of communication. How parents react to their baby's outreach for human contact impacts greatly on his emotional stability. Being held and comforted validates the infant, lets him know he is an important being, and plants the early seeds of trust, security, and love in him, which will accompany him throughout his entire life.

There isn't one simple response for every crying baby. The situation into which the baby was born needs to be taken into account. If she has a large family, a mother cannot hold a baby all day. She can, however, share the responsibility of comforting the crying infant with other members of the family, such as siblings, grandparents, the father, or a babysitter. At other times, a pacifier or swing can soothe the baby.

For some infants, however, crying tends to be a self-limiting state, one that is commonly replaced by sleep. It is important for every mother to understand that taking a break from a colicky baby benefits not only the mother and infant, but the entire family as well. It is an investment no mother can afford to neglect.

Eating

Babies spend a great deal of their waking hours eating, and there are many ways a baby eats. Some eat small quantities at a time and need more feedings. Others are content with four-hour intervals between feedings. Both types require fewer feedings as they grow older.

There are two questions that need to be explored: whether to breast-feed or bottle feed, and whether to feed the infant on demand or by schedule.

— Past and Present Views on Demand Feeding

During the 1920s and 1930s, medical authorities recommended placing the infant on a four-hour feeding schedule. John B. Watson, a leading authority at the time, felt that a child's character would be improved if his immediate needs were ignored. The trend has changed, though, and today pediatricians encourage parents to feed a baby on demand rather than by a schedule. What mothers need to realize, however, is that not every cry is an indication of hunger. Too much feeding can aggravate a sensitive stomach, while too little food can stunt the baby's physical development.

— Breast-feeding

Before 1900, there was little choice for a mother other than to nurse her baby, but by the middle of the 1940s, formula became a popular alternative to nursing. Both the medical profession and mothers chose bottle feeding over breast-feeding. Today almost every doctor recommends breast-feeding over bottle feeding, since studies have proven that breast-fed babies have many advantages over those who are bottle fed. These include a strong bond between mother and child and an arsenal of immunological benefits against allergies and infections before the infant's own antibody mechanism matures.

— Bottle Feeding

Breast-feeding is not always the answer, especially if the family is large and the demands of nursing aggravate the tension in the home. Commercial milks also tend to fill babies up more, so there are longer intervals between feedings. In addition, the father and siblings can lend a hand in the feeding process, thus allowing more time for the mother to attend to her own needs and the needs of the other members of the family, who are just as important. In addition, if a mother must take medication that is harmful to the baby, she will have no choice but to bottle feed.

No one method is the answer for every mother. Today there are choices available to help each mother decide which method of feeding is more appropriate for her and her infant. Once she has made her decision, she has no reason to feel guilty, and others should not judge her. They surely cannot know what went into her decision-making process. This is a personal and private issue that should be respected by friends and family.

Whichever mode the mother selects, she must bear in mind that intimate contact between the child and family members, especially the father, creates healthy, lifelong patterns. Perhaps more important than the debate of breast milk versus commercial milk is the issue of how much attention the infant receives. Infants need to be held, cooed, played with, and loved. These factors create a sense of security and well-being that leaves a definite favorable impact on their later emotional stability.

— As they Grow Older

As the child grows, he is introduced to solid foods and eventually weaned. But still the feeding process is a vital one. One common battle between mother and child involves eating habits. Some mothers feel they aren't being good parents unless they tell stories and play games in an effort to make the child finish every morsel of food on his plate. But most child-care professionals agree that the child should determine how much he needs to eat, not the mother.

Forcing a child to eat more than he needs can lead to obesity later in life. Simply put, a healthy child will eat what he needs. An "extra spoonful" is just that — extra (and unnecessary). On the other hand, allowing a child to binge, particularly on sweets and other junk food, not only takes away his appetite for wholesome foods, but it causes a host of physical and emotional problems.

Does this mean that never giving junk food to a child is the answer? Absolutely not. As with most things, moderation is the key. Never giving a child sweets encourages him to beg or, God forbid, steal from other children. It may cause a child to overindulge on sweets when he's old enough to be independent. A child's diet should be supervised by an adult, but flexibility is a must — a good rule for most parenting situations.

Your Infant's Health Care: Too Much Action or Too Little?

S ome mothers are slow to react regarding matters of health while others immediately panic. It is not easy to find the golden mean, as the following two stories illustrate.

I KNEW I had quite a wait ahead of me until my child would be called into the pediatrician's examining room. As we sat and waited, the mother seated next to me started a conversation. In no time, we were both laughing as we compared notes on the struggles young mothers face in dealing with their children's health care. Then my companion grew serious as she related a harrowing story of her own inexperience in the face of a serious threat to her son's well-being.

"My child was slightly over two years old," she told me, "when he received a burn on his chest. The bowl of chicken soup must have been hotter than I'd realized when he spilled it on himself. He barely cried, but upon inspection, I noticed a red blotch. I immediately put Vaseline on it, and the episode seemed over."

The mother shook her head sadly as she continued her story. "The next day, he wouldn't stop crying. Maternal instinct told me to lift up his undershirt. I froze in shock at what I saw. The innocent blotch had turned into a giant, ugly blister. I rushed him to the hospital, and the diagnosis was grim — a third-degree burn. An operation was necessary. Skin taken from his thigh was grafted onto the wound. Several weeks in the hospital, months of physical therapy, and frequent checkups at the doctor combined to make it a horrible ordeal."

Tears glistened in the woman's eyes as she went on. "All along I blamed myself. Why didn't anyone ever tell me that it's important to put cold water immediately on any burn and keep it there for at least twenty minutes? I was upset with my friends, neighbors, and even my mother. She always used oil or butter, which I now know is the worst treatment for a burn."

My heart ached for the woman and her child's misfortune, and I was relieved to hear the nurse call my child's name. For weeks I couldn't get the story out of my mind. I knew it was not really her fault. She hadn't known. How many other women act in a similar fashion, not reacting properly to a potentially serious problem?

On the other hand, overreacting can also be detrimental to your child.

A FRIEND and I were staying in the mountains. Her five-year-old came down with a fever of 102. The child was crying in discomfort. Within a few minutes the mother was on the phone to her doctor in New York.

"Can the child move her head?" he asked.

"No, no," she replied hysterically without bothering to check.

"In that case, bring her to the hospital immediately," instructed the doctor. "We must make certain it's not meningitis."

In a frenzy, my friend called a car service and threw a few necessities into a bag. Her face was flushed, and tears flowed as she envisioned the worst for her child. "Faige," I said, "you are scaring the child by overreacting to the situation. Leave the room and let me try something."

Trusting me, she left the room. From my bag I pulled out some puppets — a furry bear, a king, and a clown. I went over to the child's bed and performed my own little puppet show. Sure enough, the child stopped moaning after a few minutes, and soon she was moving her head slowly in the direction of the puppets. I moved them to the right, and her head followed. The puppets moved to the left, and, without even a whimper, the girl's head quickly followed the movement.

Ecstatic, I went outside to speak to her mother. I told my friend to call her doctor and tell him that the child could move her neck without any discomfort. The trip to the hospital was canceled, and she was spared the ordeal of many invasive and unpleasant examination procedures. By the next day the child's fever had broken and her virus diagnosed by a local doctor.

I couldn't help thinking that, as important as it is not to underreact to a child's complaints or symptoms, it's just as crucial to maintain self-control and not overreact. We are, after all, only mothers. We haven't been trained medically and often misjudge out of ignorance. It's always best to keep a cool head, remember the basics, and consult a doctor when necessary.

A healthy family needs a capable captain to run an efficient ship, one who will not let it tilt too much toward either side. A parent needs a flexible, open mind to perform the challenging task of nurturing future generations.

The Mother-Child Bond

Every mother wants her child to become a healthy mature adult. What they often do not realize is that the foundation of emotional health begins and is determined by the nurturing the infant receives during the first year of life. Each day of the first year, more cement is poured on this foundation of emotional strength. If a baby is cared for properly, the foundation is sturdy and well cemented. The stronger the foundation, the more likely the child will withstand the storms of life without major emotional residue. When a heavy storm hits a neighborhood, houses built on strong foundations are less likely to suffer damages than homes built on weak foundations. In the same way, if a baby is not cared for adequately, the perils, traumas, and life's challenges laid upon his weak foundation will most likely impact on his ability to deal with them in a strong, healthy manner. His house of emotions is much more likely to crumble under heavy stress.

Most experts on childhood disorders feel strongly that poor or inadequate emotional and physical contact between mother and infant leads to severe developmental, social, and emotional deficiencies in the first year of life that will be difficult to correct later. To ensure normal and positive separation, a child must first strongly bond to his mother.

It is from the very first attachment or relationship that a human being has with his mother and father that the child gains his impressions that influence the child when forming relationships. All adult relationships are woven to the primary attachment of infancy. If these early attachments were intense and healthy, his adult relationships will tend to be gratifying. If these early attachments were weak, inconsistent, and lacking in security, the adult may be more likely to repeatedly form similar faulty relationships.

Parents need to recognize the importance of their role. Every smile, every laugh, every diaper change, every song, every playful interaction, creates a new solid brick in a baby's foundation of life. The security and love parents give to their baby through normal physical contact and emotional interaction is almost impossible to make up for later in life. Parents should see themselves for what they are — builders of future adults. It is a role society should respect more than any career. The most successful businesswoman cannot compete with the wealth a mother imbues in her baby on a typical day.

If the mother is not emotionally or physically well, the father or other caretakers must provide additional love. Being loved is not a choice human beings have. It is a necessary ingredient in life, no less important than the oxygen we breathe.

Adults who have not received this vital intense love as a young child search for this unconditional relationship throughout their entire lives. Almost always it is fruitless and frustrating. Coercing parental love from a spouse, creating a role reversal by putting one's own child into the role of parent, demanding unrealistic gratification from friends, or masquerading as a mature adult becomes an unsuccessful journey.

The Changing Relationship in the Early Years

During the first few months of life, the infant is very self-centered and egotistical. He has little awareness of significant others in his life other than his mother. Until about five months old, the infant doesn't realize that he is a separate physical identity from the mother or primary caretaker. Infants feel enmeshed with their mother, similar to the way in which Siamese twins are connected.

At six months of age, babies realize that their mother is not attached to them and that they are individual beings. They learn that if their demand for food is not immediately met, it does not mean that they have been abandoned. By the age of eight months, the child has grasped the concept of person permanence — out of sight does not mean out of mind. The child realizes that although the mother is not in the same room with him, she is still close by. Mother will come back soon and food will be given. The child now begins to learn that he must wait — patiently or impatiently — for his needs to be met.

At six months, the baby also begins to expand his attachments to others in the family. By the time he begins to crawl and explore, he has the maturity to know that those who love him are there for him to hold him and give him what he needs when he is finished exploring. Like a turtle, he leaves his shell, but only for short periods of time. He always returns to assure himself that his mother is still there, and soon after goes off again. This game of leaving and then returning continues even after the toddler has learned to walk. Then, at about two years of age, the child begins to discover other children and stays away from his mother for longer periods of time.

The Magic Touch

It may come as a surprise to many well-meaning mothers that their own children are suffering from lack of touch. We educated, involved parents have come to associate unhappy children with those who are neglected, abused, chronically ill, or living in dysfunctional homes. However, the fact is that many children who come from good solid homes are not physically comforted, loved, nurtured, and cuddled enough.

This is because the parents themselves did not receive enough loving contact. They may not know how to cuddle, coo, kiss, and hug their children affectionately. Some mothers are unaware of how detrimental it is to habitually prop a bottle for their child to suck from rather than hold him in their arms to feed. Feeding does not just fulfill the basic need of appeasing a child's hunger; the child also needs the opportunity for close contact with the parent.

Finally, some children need more physical affection than a mother's innate personality or schedule allows. These children often fall into the category of "failure to thrive." Either at home or in school, they feel and look sad. Their expressions are blank, devoid of emotion, and their movements are limp and lethargic.

Another sign of needing to be touched is acting out by misbehaving to the point of rebellion. One ten-year-old who already had a police record confided, "I'm bad and bad until Daddy finally hits me." What the child was articulating was that a negative touch is better than no touch at all, much as a moldy piece of bread is more desirable to a starving person than no food at all.

Infants need to be held, touched, cooed, and kissed. Toddlers need tons of hugs and kisses. The best way to patch up a toddler's bruises is a kiss from Mom. When parents convey their love by being available for kisses and hugs anytime, it encourages healthy separation between mother and child.

Preschoolers need to be held in the lap, cuddled, hugged, and touched at every opportunity. A first-grader usually needs fewer hugs, but he needs them nevertheless. A mother's pat on the head, a father's holding his hand as they walk to school, all gives strong messages of love.

A ten-year-old is more difficult to hug and cuddle. Yet he, too, needs positive physical touch. When handing him an item such as an apple or book, linger an extra second to touch his hand, tousle his head. Ask permission for a hug or to be hugged.

Teenagers usually claim they don't need hugs or pats. It makes them feel babyish and silly. Don't believe them. Just be patient. Look for opportunities such as birthdays, holidays, milestones, and goodbyes for a warm hug.

The tender touch of a loved one is so immensely comforting and nurturing. It is priceless. There is no one richer than a man who can openly and appropriately display physical affection to the loved ones in his life. There is no one poorer than a man who wants to love, needs to express his love, craves love from his family, but does not know how to give or receive affection in a healthy physical manner.

The need for touch doesn't end with adulthood. It merely branches into different forms. What was once a mother's warm hug transforms into a healthy intimacy between husband and wife. What was once a father's affectionate caress transforms into an adult's healthy solid handshakes or hugs to colleagues, close friends, and siblings. Grandparents can share and thrive on the give-and-take of touch and hugs from grandchildren and their married children.

Don't think that once you're married your parents don't need your touch. They do, probably more than ever. Don't think you don't need their touch. You do, unless you are filled with unresolved childhood resentments. Touching a parent or a child should never stop regardless of age or gender. The elderly, especially those in nursing homes, probably need a warm hug or caress more than the hot food on their trays.

America, one of the richest countries in the world, is touch-starved! Our busy schedules, secondary jobs outside the home, large families, and huge responsibilities keep us on an emotional and physical marathon. Who has time to stop and think? We are glad if we make it through the day without hitting or screaming at our children. As for a hug, the child has to be sick with a high fever to get one. Otherwise, we are just too busy.

Our Western society has also made many forms of physical contact taboo. In warmer cultures, such as among North African or Sefardi Jews, no one is greeted without a kiss on both cheeks; men hug men and women hug women without hesitation or embarrassment.

YITTY, A child of six, was diagnosed with attention deficit disorder, separation anxiety, school phobia, and inability to integrate classroom material. An additional diagnosis of learning disabled soon appeared on her chart. To make matters worse, Yitty had uncontrollable screaming tantrums that got worse each month.

Three different doctors advised her parents to ignore the child's tantrums. Friends told them, "Whenever you leave the house with Yitty, takes loads of nosh along." Grandmother said Yitty's mother had been the same way as a child. It was a personality problem.

During therapy, Yitty was obsessed with bottle-feeding the dolls I keep in the office for the entire duration of the session. In the waiting room, where I went to get her, I found her with her thumb in her mouth huddled into a fetal position on one side of the bench, while her mother sat on the other side. The source of Yitty's problems became immediately clear, and I began to instruct her mother on the art of "holding therapy."

When Yitty was about to go into a tantrum, her mother was taught to hold and cuddle her until she calmed down. When Yitty was put to bed, her mother or father would hold her for ten to fifteen minutes, and upon awakening in the morning, they did another round of holding therapy. With proper instruction, Yitty's parents became the most successful therapists in the world.

Not surprisingly, within a very short time Yitty's behavior became more subdued. She had fewer tantrums, and when she did have them they were aborted by her mother or father picking her up and soothing her for fifteen minutes. Yitty gradually became a more likable child in school and at home. Her concentration increased, and she was able to absorb more classroom material.

When Pesach arrived, her grandparents came to visit.

They refused to believe that this was the same unhappy, difficult child they had always known. Just a year ago, when Yitty's father was selling the *chametz*, Yitty's four-year-old sister innocently suggested, "Why don't we sell Yitty with the *chametz*?"

Yitty was lucky. Her mother was very receptive to holding therapy. Although she herself did not receive enough of it as a child, she nevertheless allowed herself to be trained in how to provide physical nurturing. She purchased a sturdy brown rocking chair in which to rock, hold, and soothe Yitty.

The mother's efforts paid off. She related just six weeks later, "What Yitty needed was not discipline, timeout, or bribes to act like a normal six-year-old. She just needed to be held to make up for the times she was not held enough as an infant and toddler. Once I was able to satiate her need for being held, she had no problem moving to the next stage of life and was able to deal well with school, friends, learning, and play."

If we want our children to become happy, functioning adults, they must have first received a heaping helping of healthy touch from parents, friends, and grandparents. In addition, parents should be alert to signs of intrusive or abusive touch that can maim a child's personality quicker than a fire burns down a house. At no time is it all right for a child to be touched in private places. If a child complains that someone has done so, do not deny it and claim he is making it up. Believe your child. Children can make up stories about almost anything, but I have never yet seen a child make up stories about being touched intrusively in a private area of the body.

As the evidence shows, loving your child with your whole heart is not enough. A parent must know or learn how to demonstrate physical love, bearing in mind the age and stage of the child. Of course, at no point is it productive to force physical affection on anyone, nor should parents tickle a child for more than a brief second or two. Simply offer age- and stage-appropriate physical touch and be available to receive it back when your children are ready. The more a child receives healthy physical love, the more he will love the world and himself.

There Is No Substitute for a Father

While fathers are as important as mothers to the emotional welfare of infants, they may come into the picture a bit later than mothers do. This is due to the fact that it is the mother who provides most of the physical needs of the infant. Often it is when an infant begins to respond to his father's smile that bonding begins to happen. But it is important to bear in mind that there is really no specific time when this bonding takes place. For some fathers it happens the moment they set eyes on the infant; for others it may take six months or even longer. Both occurrences are normal as long as the bonding does happen at some point early in the child's life.

Many mothers are baffled at the baby's reaction when the father walks through the door. A first-time mother complained, "I do everything for my thirteen-month-old. I take care of him all day. He clings to me like a tightrope, and I feel good knowing he feels so secure with me every minute of the day. But when the lock on the door begins to turn, signaling my husband's return, he squirms out of my arms and crawls eagerly to his father. For the rest of the evening, I am ignored, feeling rejected by the baby. He only wants to be in Daddy's lap and ignores me like the plague."

I tried to explain to the mother how lucky she was that her husband and child have such a relationship. Babies need to idolize their fathers during this intense quality time in the short time their fathers are at home. Later this interactive relationship branches out to the many other stages of the child's life where a father's input is of paramount importance.

At age four, boys begin to imitate their fathers by playing shul and expressing masculine behavior by riding bikes, running, and climbing. Girls gain, too, by being loved for their femininity and getting their childish need to hear "I love you. You're beautiful..." fulfilled. While girls tend to play with dolls, they also need the physical outlets that usually the father provides, such as going to the playground and being encouraged to climb and run or learning how to ride a bike and skate.

By school age, fathers often take on an academic role, reviewing the parashah, asking questions about the *yamim tovim*. This is not instead of but in addition to the physical play between father and child.

Early childhood is also a testing time for the child, who picks up either a negative or positive relationship between his father and mother. This is not easy for the parents. In theory, they know that they must agree on all child-raising schools of thought in front of the children, but in practice it is difficult. Each parent comes from a completely different background where everything from discipline to playtime was done differently. It takes great restraint and maturity for parents not to contradict each other but rather to praise each other in front of the young scholar who is hyper-alert to the give-and-take between his parents. In all probability, this information will be stored in the subconscious until the young child marries and repeats the same form of communication he observed form his parents years ago.

When a boy reaches the ages of nine, ten, or eleven, he will be spending more time with his father than his mother — going to shul, being taken along for shopping and errands, being involved in building the sukkah, helping his father pick out the perfect *esrog*, being tested in learning, and playing ball or riding bicycles together. Along the way, the child should be showered with validation and appropriate discipline.

Girls at this age need their fathers, too, but not as much as the boys. They are usually more involved with their mother, who now becomes the center of their emulation. They love being helped with schoolwork by a calm mother, chatting about friends, and helping with the food shopping and even the cooking and baking. It is a wise mother who asks opinions of the child on small decisions such as which ingredient to put in the mixer first or which orange juice to buy. The best time to have both parents interact with both the boys and girls is during mealtimes, *simchahs*, and family occasions such as birthdays.

This separation of parent identification continues to widen as children become teenagers. On one hand, they need the same kind of attention from both parents as they did in the early years — validation, conversation, physical fun such as swimming and walks, and, of course, keen interest in what the child is learning, his rebbes, and friends. On the other hand, the girl spends more of her time with her mother and a boy spends more of his time with his father.

When people ask which children are more likely to be at risk, I always have my answer ready: "The ones who do not have a good relationship with both their parents." (Of course there are children who are at risk in spite of having gotten the correct dose of parental guidance. For this reason, we must always daven to Hashem to steer our children in the right direction.)

When a child marries, the parent-child relationship affects the marital relationship. If it was good, the couple's relationship will be good. If the parent-child relationship was fragmented before the marriage, chances are it will overlap into the husband-wife relationship.

Some fathers might say, "Hey, you are expecting a lot from me." My response to them is, "What you put in is what you take out. The choice is yours."

To Work or Not to Work?

Working mothers often come to my office, worried that they are unfit mothers. They feel guilty and ashamed for having to work to help pay expenses.

Being a working mother myself for eighteen of the twenty years I have been married, I can say, without hesitation, if you don't have to work, don't! The mother, not a substitute, is usually the one who is best equipped to care for her children.

However, this choice is not available to every mother, as it was not to me. I did not have the luxury of choosing to work or stay home. I had to work. Believe me, it was not easy, especially when my children were babies. I always dreaded leaving my nursing baby with a babysitter and never got used to it. I hated parting with my baby each morning and often cried the entire way to work. I worried that I had forgotten something my baby might need. It was important to me that my babies have breast milk, not formula, and I put in a lot of effort to ensure that they did.

Did I remember to take my portable milk pump along? Did I pack the sterilized bottle? Did I leave enough milk for the baby? These thoughts invaded my morning walk to work. When I arrived, I made an effort to put aside my personal pain and concentrated on doing my job of teaching preschool. Luckily, I loved my job, the job loved me, and the challenging day passed quickly for me. On the way home, I thought again of my baby at the babysitter's and felt a stab of regret zigzag through my heart. I had to control myself to keep from running to get my baby.

The minute I got home, I kissed my baby nonstop until he squirmed in my arms. Then I would relax in my recliner and nurse the hungry baby with songs, cooing, and loving words. For me, no experience in the world compared to the joy of nurturing my own baby. The phone rang, the doorbell buzzed, the oven timer beeped, but I ignored it all. I was cozy and snug, dozing as the baby blissfully nursed to his content.

But too soon for comfort, the fantasy where only baby love, bonding, feeding, and napping existed was over, and the real world rushed upon me like a tidal wave. Quickly take the supper out of the oven, make a grocery list, do three loads of laundry, and call the plumber to repair a broken pipe. All had to be done before the older children and my husband walked through the door. Reluctantly, I got up to get to work at my second job, my household duties.

I didn't want another job. I only wanted to be a housewife and mother. I didn't need validation to know that it was the most important job in the world. I knew that mothering was a privilege given to me four times over, and no one could do the job as well as I. I also felt accomplished, knowing I was raising the next generation of *klal Yisrael*.

Why, then, did I work? I wanted to be a supermom and excel at all fronts. I wanted my husband to learn in *kollel* for at least a year. Later I wanted him to learn a trade. Little did I know that the trade would take six years to learn. In the meantime, Hashem had blessed us with children to feed, rent to pay, tuition to meet, clothes to buy. Since the bliss of Torah learning did not yield financial income, nor did learning a trade, I had no choice but to work outside the home. Too bad no one offered to support us in this interim; I would have grabbed the chance.

While I do understand that there are women with young children who work for pleasure, I have not met too many of them. Most working mothers I come across work because they have to help their husbands meet the financial needs of the average family. It almost seems you have to be rich to stay home, especially if your babies need Pampers, toddler needs a play group, first-grader needs a tutor for reading, fifth-grade daughter wants to go to camp with the rest of her class, teenager's clothes cost as much as yours do, your son's dorming mesivta tuition costs as much as your mortgage, and your eldest daughter is being offered a match to a yeshivah boy who wants to be supported for five years, minimum.

A working mother does not by any means put her child at risk, neither spiritually nor emotionally. On the contrary, often these children are more likely to become responsible and mature adults. The mother working outside the home only makes successful parenting twice as hard for both mother and father. So when a woman has to find a job, I say, "Welcome to the ranks of supermom runners who race against the clock seven days a week."

Shabbos preparations begin when energy allows it to. If Sunday night you get a surge of energy to bake challos, you grab the opportunity and freeze them.

You prepare dinner every night within fifteen minutes with your *sheitel* still on your head, high heels still on your feet. Changing into more comfortable attire takes a minute you don't have when hungry voices chant, "When will supper be ready? I'm starving."

If you think your day is over when supper is, brace yourself. With homework to help the kids with, calls to return, dishes to wash, children's stories to listen to, and a husband who craves moral support after a long day at the office or *kollel*, you wish you had the flu so you could escape to bed with a good reason.

One exasperated working mother was angry at the media for portraying working mothers in so negative a light. She said, "Except for the few who are running away from their home responsibilities, the answer is we work because we have to. Life today is such that it demands two incomes to cover basic necessities. It isn't fair to lay guilt on the majority of us who are sacrificing our roles to help pay bills because of those few women who run out of the house because they hate being mothers."

I nodded with agreement as she continued, "Ideally, if I had it my way, I would work a few hours a day to stimulate my mind and relish the joys of motherhood the rest of the time. But since life isn't always ideal, I will continue to work long hours and fantasize that an invisible angel is doing my dishes while I'm doing the homework of four different grade levels."

When I finally do fall into bed, I say Shema with full concentration. I thank Hashem for giving me the strength to do what most of our grandparents didn't have to do: choose between staying home — and not being able to pay tuition — or going to work and crying all along the twenty-minute walk to and from work.

I can hear my grandmother whispering comforting words in my ears: "Shhh, don't talk so loud. Working outside the home is an individual and personal decision. People have different needs and circumstances. When you can't have the best, you often have to settle for second best."

Too bad you aren't here now, Bubby Sara. With your wisdom, you would have found the proper words to empathize with the struggles of the working mother while appreciating the joy of the mother who has the luxury of staying home to raise her children.

The Baby Sale

WE ALL know how precious and priceless a newborn baby is, but one day this was brought home to me most dramatically. I knew of a Jewish baby that commanded a price of over forty thousand dollars, and this was considered a bargain.

Yaffa had long bleached-blond hair with streaks of black peaking out at the scalp. It blanketed her entire back, and half of her face was covered with thick fierce bangs that mingled with protruding fake eyelashes. I wondered how she was able to see and soon discovered Yaffa's secret. She had a habit of alternating between deep-throated puffs from her cigarette to nervous right-handed swings of her bangs, pushing them to the side of her face.

Observing Yaffa sitting in the chair across from mine, I couldn't help wondering what her issue was. If she was on drugs, I would refer her to a drug rehabilitation clinic. If she was homeless, I would refer her to social services for welfare. Whatever her problem was, I was sure it was not for me to handle. Since I was only a student at the time, doing my internship, I knew that offering long-term counseling and therapy to someone who needs immediate social services or is in the midst of a crisis is not a good idea. A starving man needs a hot bowl of soup, not a discussion on how he can regain his dignity. Besides, Yaffa didn't look like my typical *heimishe* client, and I was almost relieved to direct her to sources that could be of better help to her than my therapeutic discussions.

Much to my surprise, Yaffa wasn't seeking Medicaid or any social services. She explained in Hebrew mingled with broken English that she had a dilemma and needed a social worker. She said she had dealt with American banks and in fact was a business lady. She had come to consult me about her business venture.

I cut Yaffa off before she could continue and explained that I was no business expert. What she needed was a business consultant, not a therapist. But Yaffa refused to take no for an answer. She continued to blow clouds of smoke into my face and repeatedly expose her eyes as she begged me to hear her out. I sat back in my chair, ready to listen. After all, Yaffa was a Jewish soul, and I wasn't about to throw her out if she needed to talk, regardless of the topic.

"I just had a baby," she blurted out, "and I don't know what to do with him."

Instantly my adrenaline shot up. "When did you give birth?" I interrupted.

"Two days ago. I gave birth to a little boy at home."

I gasped. The ten million questions crowding my mind had to wait. Controlling my urge to quiz her, I simply nodded gently, prodding her on.

"I'm Jewish," she continued with pride. "I had a real Jewish wedding on the beach just last summer." Her eyes opened wide, and a smile broadened her pale wide face as she continued with drama, "My husband married me on a gorgeous summer night. The water was our witness, and the stars were the guests that blessed us with much happiness. My husband said the moon was the shining pious rabbi that graced our wedding."

I almost lost my composure and asked what medication she was on, but I did not want to break the spell of her good mood. I needed information if I was going to ensure the safety of the baby. Wishing her "*Mazel tov*" with a forced smile, I asked where the baby was.

My patience paid off. Yaffa explained that the baby was home with her girlfriend. Her husband had flown to Israel a week before she gave birth. I gently asked how I could help her as I handed her a plastic cup to serve as an ashtray. Her face suddenly turned sly with childish glee. I wondered how old she really was behind the long bleached hair and false lashes.

Yaffa didn't procrastinate long. She explained that a car service was waiting for her outside and she was in a hurry. The baby had not yet received a medical checkup, nor did he have a home to live in. Originally a nice *frum* family by the name of Abramowitz were supposed to take the baby. They even paid for her doctors and expenses. However, they changed their mind when they realized that in addition to being a chain smoker Yaffa drank. Yaffa swore in a stream of tears that during the pregnancy she had not smoked a single cigarette nor drank a single glass of vodka.

I wondered how she had maintained such strict self-discipline. As if she had read my mind, she said, "Do you know the Rosensheins from Boro Park?"

I did. I also knew that they had adopted a beautiful

little girl three years ago and thanked Hashem every day for their bundle of joy who was about to start kindergarten.

"Well, their baby girl is mine. I carried her in my stomach for nine months." She oozed with sheer *nachas*. "For fifty thousand dollars, I could stop drinking and smoking. My babies are guaranteed to be healthy. But the Abramowitzes changed their minds, and now I am stuck with a new baby and no money to go home. I want to go back to Israel as soon as possible, but first I must do something with the baby."

Yaffa wondered if a Jewish agency would pay for her baby. If one of our Jewish agencies such as the one I was working at paid her, she would rather put the baby in a nice Jewish home.

Before I could catch my breath, Yaffa was stubbing out her cigarette unto my desktop, ignoring the plastic cup I had given her for that purpose. Nervously she threw a piece of paper with her phone number into my lap.

The next minute she was gone.

In a daze, I stared at her phone number, recognizing from the first three digits that she lived in Flatbush. More than that was a mystery. I trembled at the responsibility she had thrust on me. The clock said it was time to go home, but I knew that if I did tomorrow would be too late. Yaffa seemed desperate. By the next day the baby might be discharged to a non-Jewish agency, forever lost to his Jewish heritage.

Whom should I call? The rabbi who rules on difficult issues for us social workers? I dialed his number but received a recording to call in three hours. I contemplated calling the police but disconnected before they picked up, afraid they might complicate things more than help.

Ohel. Yes, that was a good idea. Surely they came across such situations more often than I. I flipped through my Rolodex for the orphanage's number and never made it past the letter *O*. By chance the Rolodex stopped at the name Peretz. I turned the Rolodex backward to *O* and this time turned it too fast. The Rolodex turned around completely and once again stopped at the name Peretz.

Was this a coincidence? A sign from God? Who were the Peretzes anyway? I couldn't even remember them. Quickly I checked the old files to see if there was a file with that name, and, sure enough, under *P* I found Peretz. With great curiosity, I opened the file and discovered an amazing story.

In July 1986, when another social worker had occupied my office, a family by the name of Peretz had undergone a tremendous tragedy. Their baby girl, twelve weeks old, died of sudden infant death syndrome. The parents were devastated beyond hope. They could not have other children. Due to uncontrollable hemorrhaging during the pregnancy, an emergency hysterectomy had to be performed to save Mrs. Peretz's life twenty-four hours after the birth. Now she didn't even have hope of having another child to make up for the loss of the infant taken so abruptly and innocently.

The last entry, dated August 19, 1986, stated that Mrs. Peretz had plunged into deep depression, bordering on a nervous breakdown. A psychiatrist from Beth Israel Mental Health had taken over the case.

Mrs. Greensweig, the social worker who had handled

the situation, was someone I knew. I called her immediately and luckily found her at home. Yes, she remembered the story clearly. The Peretzes were a darling chassidic couple. They were pillars of the community, helping everyone in need regardless of the situation or family. Mrs. Peretz had long recovered from her depression and now served as the coordinator of the volunteers to Chronic Disease Hospital. Three times a day she made the trip to feed the feeble and see to it that all patients were fed.

"Would they be interested in a newborn Jewish baby?" I asked.

Mrs. Greensweig grew more and more excited as I related the episode involving Yaffa to her. Yes, she was almost sure they would love to adopt a healthy Jewish baby. Who wouldn't in their situation? And if they didn't, she knew at least five couples offhand who desperately wanted to love and raise a baby. Newborn babies were very difficult to come by, especially a Jewish one. Mrs. Greensweig offered to call the Peretzes and feel them out, and I was instructed to call Yaffa immediately and tell her that we were taking the baby one way or another.

My head was whirling with a blend of excitement and fear. What if Yaffa wasn't home? What if the baby was already gone? My fingers trembled as I pushed the buttons and mumbled two verses of Tehillim.

Yaffa was home, but she did not want to speak to me. She briskly explained that she no longer needed my services. The Italian next door had heard about her plight and were nice enough to offer her twenty-five thousand dollars in cash plus a one-way first-class ticket to Israel on the early-morning flight.

"Yaffa," I cried with desperation, "please do not sell your baby to a non-Jew!"

But Yaffa had hung up. Apparently she didn't want to hear my arguments. Apparently the offer of twenty-five thousand dollars was more valuable to her than religion. Too broken to do anything, I gave in to the lump in my throat and broke out in cries of anguish.

The phone rang, and I almost didn't hear it through my volcanic sobs. My mind was racing. Six million Jews perished in the Holocaust, and now another soul was about to be snuffed out.

Finally, I grabbed the phone. It was Mrs. Greensweig. Her voice was filled with excitement. The Peretzes would love to adopt a Jewish baby. It would be a lifelong dream come true.

I didn't want to break the bad news, but I couldn't hold on to it either. "The baby is sold," I choked into the phone, and I repeated my conversation with Yaffa.

"Call her back quick! Tell her you'll give her forty thousand tonight plus a first-class ticket to Israel for tomorrow."

My adrenaline shot up again, but I reined in my emotions. I didn't believe it was possible to get hold of forty thousand dollars in one hour. People did not keep that kind of cash around, and all the banks were closed.

"Forget it," I murmured. "It's too late. We can't do the impossible. I suppose it was *bashert* this way."

Mrs. Greensweig was furious and argued that it was not too late. There were lots of wealthy people who kept money in vaults. The Peretzes had contacts in the community. Many people had access to money via ATM machines. "They will respond," she insisted. "I'm sure of it.

If necessary, we will hire people to make public appeals the way they make public announcements — through a loudspeaker on top of cars. Call her back right now and tell her that we will be there in an hour with the cash, the new parents, and a lawyer."

I called, but I didn't sound like any businesslady. I meekly told Yaffa that a Jewish family had forty thousand dollars in cash and they could bring it over within the hour. I heard her gurgling laughter and felt like a fool. My heart agreed with Yaffa that the mission was impossible, but like me she said vaguely, "Okay. Be here in an hour with the money, and you can take the baby."

She gave me her address and hung up chuckling. I could just see her shaking her head of long blond hair in wonder.

Not wanting to feel like a fool but unable to get out of the mess, I gave Mrs. Greensweig the address and drove at a turtle's pace to the address in Flatbush. Yaffa opened the door, and immediately I could see that they were not there yet. I hesitated and then apologized, because the hour was almost up. Yaffa just shrugged her shoulders and said, "I'm used to being disappointed. Don't be surprised if they don't show up."

The next thing I knew, Yaffa was thrusting a baby into my arms. In shock, I lost my equilibrium and almost tripped with the baby in tow. There it was, the most expensive item money could possibly buy right in my arms. He looked like an angel, sleeping contentedly in a torn yellow stretchy that pushed his front toes into the open. Instinctively, I bent down to kiss his exposed toes and instantly fell in love with the two-day-old angel.

"I want him," I murmured, and Yaffa laughed again.

"It's not easy to make money these days. One must do what one must to put food into one's mouth. I had three babies for money, but my husband took half of it, and I've already spent what I had. But I'm not doing it again. It's too hard to stop drinking and smoking. Besides, the next one I want for myself. I need someone to take care of me when I get old. Tomorrow he goes to the Mantinis, and I'm going —"

The bell rang, and Yaffa paled as she whispered, "You think they really came? I would much rather have him grow up in a Jewish home. Believe me, it's not the fifteen-thousand-dollar difference. My father and my husband are both *kohanim* —"

"Get the bell!" I begged. "We'll talk later."

Later never came. In strode a crew of strangers who identified themselves as Mr. and Mrs. Peretz, Philip Green, the lawyer, and Mrs. Greensweig. I felt as if I was in an unbelievable dream and was sure that soon I'd wake up to tell my kids about it.

Mr. Green took charge. He had the papers ready to be signed. He read Yaffa her rights and then handed the bulk of papers to the Peretzes to sign. Mrs. Greensweig and I cosigned as witnesses. Immediately Mr. Peretz handed Yaffa a huge shopping bag filled with cash. We all stood around, tense and impatient, while Yaffa counted the money. It took her over an hour. What was in reality about sixty minutes seemed like a lifetime as the seconds slowly ticked by. Mr. Peretz began davening from a Tehillim. Mrs. Peretz was biting her lips and nails alternately. Mrs. Greensweig nervously paced in circles. I rocked the baby gently, more from jitters than necessity, while cooing over and over, "Don't worry. Everything will be fine."

Philip Green was the only one who kept his composure, telling us all to calm down. We promised we would, but none of us did. Not until Yaffa sighed and said it was over. The money was all there, forty thousand dollars in cash. On cue, Mrs. Peretz took the baby from my arms and quickly hurried out. Everyone followed suit. Yaffa called out, "Take good care," and hastened to close the door.

In silence, I watched them pour into Mr. Green's car just as the door to the house opened again, and Yaffa yelled, "My ticket! My ticket! You forgot to give me my ticket to Israel!"

Mr. Green mumbled, "I'm sorry," and handed her the ticket.

Their car sped away, and I walked toward my car in a daze, still convinced that I was in a dream. I got home very late. After apologizing to my family, I sat down as if by remote control and ate supper. Then I called my supervisor and told her the story. She was in shock and berated me for not calling her earlier. Deep down I knew she was right, but at that point, I didn't really care. As a student, I could get away with anything. I went to sleep, waiting to wake up from my dream. It's been three years now, and I'm still waiting.

Today I received a phone call. It was Mrs. Peretz. Beautiful and healthy little Baruch was turning three years old and having his *upsherin*. Would I please come to share in the *simchah*? Memories of the many small miracles that spun together to create such an unbelievable story forced me to admit that when Hashem orchestrates a dream, you never have to wake up from it. Dreams do come true. Like miracles, Hashem can make them happen any minute. And where there's a healthy, loving heart pining for a child, Hashem can perform miracles to find that child and bring him home.

2 to 4 Years

Autonomy versus Shame and Doubt

Children are curious. Born explorers, they crawl, walk, and climb to satisfy their curiosity. At the same time, they are faced with the limit-setting of parents. When parents provide ample room for independent growth while patiently establishing appropriate boundaries, children acquire a sense of independence and competence.

If children are too restricted and not allowed to explore the world, they may develop an excessive sense of shame and doubt.

Those who climb a mountain would do well to sit down first with binoculars and survey the terrain to select the best path for reaching their desired goal. Then he picks the most effective ropes, crampons, and axes and starts out with direction and purpose...and so it is with discipline.

— Naomi Brill

Balancing Control
and Freedom

At age two the child no longer depends only on physical gratification — eating, sucking, cooing, and intimate physical contact — for his emotional and physical health. He has the developmental maturity to be locomotive and to reach out to significant others rather than being dependent on their coming to him. He can walk and explore the world with awe and at the same time return to siblings and caretakers for hugs, love, and attention. The two main issues a child between the ages of two and four faces is juggling his need for independence and toilet training.

Discipline varies as the child matures and gains a deeper understanding of wrong and right. Power struggles between parent and two-year-old in the form of temper tantrums should have eased up as the child grows older and better able to communicate, since the child now has the verbal maturity to negotiate his emotional needs and does not need to resort to physically aggressive behavior. School-age children who have a basic schedule — morning routines, school, supper, homework, play, and a bedtime hour — thrive emotionally on the predictability of their day if they are also allowed to make age-appropriate choices, such as deciding which of two dresses may be worn, whether to brush teeth before or after getting undressed, or which homework assignment to do first.

The key point to remember is that the routine of the day stays the same, but decision-making on how to carry it out can be implemented by the children. This gives them room to develop their individuality, while providing predictability, a major ingredient of emotional security.

When Parents Are Too Lenient

Children who lack structure in the routine of the day due to parental guilt, ignorance, or inability to remain consistent often find themselves in reverse roles. Instead of the parents controlling the behavior of the child and the routine of the house, the child becomes the power figure who controls the parents and the entire household.

Giving so much power to a child who does not have the maturity to handle it is like electing a ten-year-old president. Who in his right mind would vote for a ten-year-old to run the country? What would happen to the armed forces, national budget, and crime? The country would be in a state of chaos in a very short time. Yet many parents are doing just that by empowering their children with authority to set the structure and limits in the home.

To make matters worse, children lose more and more of their self-confidence as their parents allow them more and more freedom. A house devoid of daily routine does not create emotionally healthy children. It is no wonder that an unstructured schedule creates undisciplined children who cannot carry out long-term goals. They are too easily distracted and frustrated to stay with one project for long. As adults they suffer, having failed to attain the proper skills to delay instant gratification in exchange for long-term gains. Most disturbing, perhaps, is the problem of poor adult self-restraint in controlling anger, invading the physical privacy of others, and not taking into account the consequences of doing or taking what is incorrect according to law or religion.

Children cannot do everything that adults can do. They cannot foresee and plan as adults can, for they lack the experience in living to do so correctly. Some of the most serious childhood anxieties comes from the failure of parents to set limits to a child's impulsive behavior, providing wise guidance and discipline when indicated. A child is not born with self-control; this ability has to be learned.

(Cameron Rychiak, *Personality Disorders*)

Too much power can also instill fear. Children need a basic schedule that tells them when meals take place, until when they can play, when to do homework, and when to go to sleep. Allowing children to create their own structure is like leaving them in a house all alone emotionally. They will be afraid of themselves, be unable to handle new emotions, and get jittery at every unfamiliar noise. When there is no structure, it is as if the mother has gone away and will never come home.

Poor child! He stands at the window waiting, but there is no one to rescue him. Mother, the disciplinary figure who represents security, is gone. Who will tell him that the noises outside are safe? Who will tell him what is good to eat and what is not? Who will tell him what to do if a fire starts? No one. He has only himself, the ego of a young undeveloped child, immature and scared to handle adult issues.

When Parents Are Too Strict

Children don't need to be supervised every minute either. It is stifling and represses their need for emotional growth. The best avenue therefore is to create a strong schedule or structure for the child, but to allow him to make decisions within that structure.

Parents who go to the opposite extreme by controlling too much of the child's activities and choices instill the same insecurities into their children as too-lenient parents. A child who is not given the freedom to choose his toys or clothes becomes dependent on adults to make decisions for him. He does not acquire the know-how to correct mistakes and make choices in daily matters. He remains stuck in an infantile emotional stage. Just as a two-month-old wouldn't know whether to use crayons or Magic Markers to paint a poster, so too, a five-year-old who was always told how to do everything will be unable to decide between the Magic Markers or the crayons.

If parents resort to too much physical punishment, children will not improve their behavior. On the contrary, the disciplinary measure will backfire as soon as the child finds another child younger or smaller to hit back at. He couldn't hit his parents back, but he surely can hurt others.

Aggressive personality disorders and antisocial personality disorders are most often created by parents who have used physical punishment to an excess. The child who lives in a physically or emotionally chaotic environment feels out of control. The only way he can gain control is by forcing his needs, impulsivity, and aggression onto others. Both the children of too lenient or too strict parents face the same dangers of imposing their will onto others by force when they become adults.

On the other hand, a child of too-strict parents may grow into a submissive adult, often resulting in dependency disorders. Thus two siblings raised in the same too-strict environment may grow to have opposite personality disorders. One may become the person people are apt to take advantage of, and the other may become the person who always seeks to take advantage of others.

It takes an emotionally healthy adult to discipline with love, while at the same time to restrain the impulse to control her children and to allow a child to learn from his mistakes. More than anything, children during this stage need to have their magnificent grandiosity appreciated and yet their failures accepted and understood. When parents cannot do so, children pretend and assume a pseudo personality to please their parents.

Toilet Training

Nature's Way

Years ago, when disposable diapers were not yet invented, parents tended to toilet-train toddlers earlier than today. Often as early as eight months old, when the child was able to sit well, the potty was introduced and the baby was made to sit for hours until he voided.

Today professionals frown on such premature methods that succeeded in toilet training the child by two years of age. Now parents are more relaxed and allow the child to show signs of readiness before toilet training. This works well most of the time, since the typical child by age two begins to be repulsed by his own dirty diaper. Waiting for the child to indicate that he desires toilet training as opposed to the mother pushing it means an easy and peaceful transition from diaper to toilet.

Mother's Way

Not every mother has the patience to wait for the child to indicate readiness. She may already have two other babies in diapers and is overwhelmed with the task of being a "diapering machine." She may prefer to encourage and praise the laid-back two-year-old. With consistent effort, the child eventually learns to use the toilet. This is fine as long as there is no feeling of pressure or disapproval involved. If the child balks at gentle efforts, it is best to wait a few months before trying again. Tension centering on toilet issues can lead to chronic constipation later on. A mother who toilet-trained her child too early wins the battle, but loses the war. The scars of the battle lie dormant, waiting for adulthood to shed its tears.

While there is no one answer for everyone, parents need to keep in mind that being toilet-trained is often not in the control of the child. One cannot teach an infant to operate a typewriter, not only because he lacks the cognitive ability, but because his motor coordination as well as his ability to follow instructions has not yet developed. In the same vein, some children gain the developmental maturity to control bowel movements earlier than others. To punish a child whose control development is sluggish compared to other siblings may cause long-term neuroses and personality disorders.

Teaching Morality to Youngsters

A child under the age of two has little awareness of the needs of others. His basic moral philosophy is "What's mine is mine, but what's yours is mine, too." He cannot seriously take into account the feelings and needs of others. Even at age three, it is very common for children to steal from their peers, not because they are bad, but because they cannot fully differentiate between what belongs to them and what belongs to others. Their immature cognitive ability cannot comprehend that taking what is not theirs is wrong. They imagine that anything within physical reach is theirs just because they can reach it.

But parents should not take a laid-back attitude and wait for a child's morality to develop on its own. It won't happen. Caretakers must explain the concept of stealing until the child comprehends the message through verbal communication and positive reinforcement — punishing him when he does something wrong and rewarding him when he refrains from wrongdoing.

But punishing a child for an act in which he doesn't yet understand the consequences may result in long-term negative effects on the child. Often the child will do privately what he cannot do publicly. The best form of teaching correct social behavior is role modeling. In addition, explain in simple words what stealing is and that it is incorrect behavior. Reward the child when he does an honest action.

When punishment is kept to a minimum, children will copy positive behavior before they are even able to talk. Pediatric specialists Piaget and Kolberg emphasize that by seeing parents behave in a moral way children will most often mimic them even before fully grasping the reasons for doing so. Piaget termed this reaction "moral realism." He states:

Gradually children come to appreciate that there are reasons for behavior. They also discover that it is possible to feel that an action is wrong or bad before knowing why it is so.

A classic example is a mother who bumps her arm and says, "Ouch, it hurts." A toddler who has been properly nurtured and witnessed his mother caring for others will most likely empathize by repeating "Ouch!" and then promptly gives his mother a soothing kiss on her arm.

One of the most essential responsibilities parents have to children is to teach them morality, religious rituals, and proper social interaction, such as caring for the needy. However, some parents, in their eagerness to raise future tzaddikim, begin the task intensely and vigorously at a very early age. While exposure to good and moral behavior is never too early for any child, teaching religious practices such as saying a blessing before eating has to be age appropriate. Forcing a child to perform religious rituals before his maturity or comprehension has developed is fruitless and often detrimental.

A four-year-old should be encouraged to say his daily prayers; however, the child should not be punished if he does not wish to cooperate. A two-year-old who refuses to say a blessing prior to eating her ice cream or only recites a partial one should not be reprimanded by having her ice cream taken away from her. Instead of noticing what she hasn't done, focus on and validate the small religious rituals she has done, even if they aren't perfect. Encouragement and behavioral demonstrations are the best ways to promote enthusiastic and joyful religious practice later in life.

Why Is My Child Afraid?

FAIGE IS four years old and replete with phobias. She is afraid of going to school, afraid the bus will crash when it finally brings her home, gets nightmares, bites her nails, and at times crinkles the edge of her skirt unconsciously but obsessively. Mother leaving the house becomes a common trauma.

Her brother Benjy is just the opposite. He fears nothing and no one. He climbs gates ten feet tall and demands a picture before getting down. He was once left on the school bus. Hours later, when he was finally discovered, his mother looked like she had been resuscitated from the dead. Benjy was calm and wanted to know what the fuss was about. "I knew the bus had to pick up kids tomorrow," he said, "so I just went to sleep." That was it. No lingering fear or trauma. The next day he had no problem getting on the bus, but his sister Faige did. She was afraid that today she would be left on the bus.

Nature versus Nurture

Why is one child so fearful and the other so brave? Is it

nature or is it nurture that makes children so different from each other?

The truth is, both factors play big roles in the secure or insecure disposition of the child. Some children are simply born with strong emotional armor. They can experience a natural disaster or personal calamities and appear unaffected or only slightly affected by them. They just don't scare easily. This nature is innate and protects them like an armor protects a knight. This personality is a blessing just as a talent is a gift from God.

On the other side of the spectrum is the child whose emotional armor is full of holes and who is concerned that swords will penetrate through the holes any minute and bring devastating catastrophes on him, perhaps even death. No wonder he screams when his protector, his mother, leaves. He now becomes more vulnerable to the hazards of the world. The many holes in his armor make him genuinely afraid, and it isn't easy to patch holes made in steel.

It takes a sensitive mother to empathize with the fearful child without unconsciously agreeing that indeed the world is a fearful place. It then takes patience and know-how to teach him to cement shut the holes in his armor.

Not every mother can do this alone. Often she may need the intervention of professionals who deal with this phenomenon on a daily basis. Which mothers seek advice? Those who are secure in their role of mother and realize that not everything is within their control. Some personality traits are inborn but can be helped — if help is sought.

The Unbroken Chain of Fear

Children's radars are often more sensitive than we are aware of. They pick up parental dispositions such as depression, fear, anger, and happiness like magnets pick up nails. A mother who is doing her best to hide her anxiety over her mother's illness, for example, may find that her child is suddenly anxious about going to school or sleeping alone in a room. She may not even make a connection between the two anxieties, hers and that of the child.

For this reason, it is often better to address the children about a family problem rather than try to hide it completely. Children will pick up vibes that something happened. If the matter is concealed from them, immediately their imaginations will begin to snowball until they have built a story greater than a mountain of snow. Usually their story is a lot worse than the real events.

For this reason, mothers should tell the child something about an anxiety provoking situation. The something can be part of the story or an explanation with a positive outlook, such as expressing belief in Hashem or suggesting the child give a penny each day for *tzedakah* or recite a verse of Tehillim. When the child is involved on a level he can understand, there is no need for him to fabricate horror stories.

There may be no trauma that causes the children anxiety, but they are picking up their parents' personalities. Children often are reflections of parents' characters. It is a good idea to ponder whether a child's trait is not similar to one's own traits. A mother who is inclined to be nervous may find that her children are nervous as well. A mother who screams a lot will find her children screaming at siblings and friends. The father who hits before thinking will have children who do the same.

On the positive side, a calm mother usually has calm children. A mother who is sensitive to others will find her children being sensitive to the needs of their friends and the needs of parents and siblings.

An honest parent who can look at her children's personalities and see if they are negatively reflecting her own may come up with answers that can be addressed and resolved for both parent and child.

The Traumatized Child

Much as parents want to protect their children from all illnesses and catastrophes, they can't. Life often brings trials and tribulations and does not discriminate against children. It therefore can be a big challenge for parents to just sit back and offer nothing more than support to children in times of serious illness, crisis, or calamity. Children often have the misconception that Mommy and Daddy can do anything. When the realization hits the child that parents cannot do everything to protect him, that they are not always in control, the child may abruptly lose his security and experience emotional trauma.

If a second trauma then takes place, if the child becomes seriously ill, for instance, he will find it difficult to deal with the pain, strangers, or a frightening environment such as a hospital. The most effective way to diminish the trauma is to be with the child as often as possible. It is for this reason that most parents do not leave a child alone for any given amount of time during a hospital stay. The more support the parents offer, the less likely that emotional scars will develop into future phobias.

Some phobias are residues of a trauma experienced by the child that was unnoticed by the parent, such as a child's reactions to an injured sibling, youngsters experiencing a scary episode such as a house robbery, or a child not properly prepared for the absence of his mother when she goes to give birth.

A child may be afraid to express his fears and be consoled because he thinks he would be contradicting his parents' philosophy. When a child hears his mother saying, "Thank God, it was only stitches, not surgery," about his sibling's injury, he may take that as a message that he is not supposed to be afraid. He will suppress his fear rather than talk it out.

The grandmother who has come to tend the children when their mother goes to give birth will express her excitement when she makes calls to convey the news, but the young two- or three-year-old doesn't share the excitement. Being told that Mommy will come back in a week does not necessarily console a child who doesn't understand the concept of time. For a young child, a week may mean forever.

The child who hears his parents' gratitude that a crisis did not turn into a disaster may not be as thankful as they are. His immature emotions cannot view the traumatic period as over or say, "Thank God it wasn't worse." The episode lingers on in dreams and shakes his emotional stability. He feels dumb speaking to Mommy about something she considers over and done with.

The child deals with the trauma by repressing it. Later it can turn into full-blown post–traumatic stress syndrome, complete with depression, anxiety, and/or phobias. If you see signs of post–traumatic stress syndrome, it would be wise to seek professional help to identify the trauma and help the child get it out of his system for once and for all.

Excessive Exposure to Fearful Stimuli

Most parents are aware that hearing scary stories, listening to frightening tapes, or overhearing too much adult conversation may be frightening to a child. What they don't realize is how strongly children are affected, even by just one fairy tale or news report. Children may imitate the characters that frighten them or reenact the horror stories in an attempt to do away with the fear.

The clinical term for this is *reaction formation*. To ward off the fearful person, children become two people. One part of them frightens others by bullying and using violence. Another part of them is fearful of mundane things or exaggerates normal events into fears. Both traits can coexist in one child.

An example of this is a child who hurts his peers without fear of consequences but worries excessively about harm to himself. He is afraid to sleep in the dark, panics at the first sound of thunder, or worries that someone will kidnap him from the schoolyard. What this child may be conveying is a fragile sense of identity that is overwhelmed by too much fearful stimuli. When hearing about men shooting each other on the news, it appears macho at first but leaves a lingering fear that one day the same man will come to his schoolyard and shoot the children, himself included.

Too much exposure to fearful events too early in life contributes to an enormous amount of unnecessary fear. Just one scary story can leave imprints of insecurity that grows with the child. Rarely does a child outgrow fearful exposure.

For this reason, teachers of young children should be cautioned on how to teach parts of the Torah that are difficult for children to comprehend. Using props such as a knife or bending a child's neck backward to demonstrate the *akeidah* is more emotionally detrimental than academically beneficial. Parents should take an active part in ensuring that certain portions of the Torah be taught at a later age or on a level that is positive and constructive.

Fear comes in all shapes and sizes. Do what you can to protect your child from fearful exposure. Life is challenging enough without having to add to it prematurely.

Limit-Setting Is a Must!

Many children are getting all the attention they need and even more. Yet they are not happy or secure. Much to the surprise of their teachers and parents, they are never satisfied. As soon as one need is met, they ask for something else. And the wish must be gratified immediately. These children have no capacity to wait for rewards or to delay gratification. They want everything *now*!

This pattern repeats in cycles from morning to night. Very often the parents are well-meaning, wonderful people who would sacrifice for their children and do. Still, the child is unhappy, demanding, insecure, anxious, and manipulative. One four-year-old child with this personality can keep two sets of parents busy all day and still remain unsatisfied. The parents realize that something is wrong yet feel like a spider trapped in its own web.

Perhaps the first point to remember is that it is not the child's fault. Rules and regulations were not adequately incorporated into the child's life.

All babies are born selfish and demanding. While this is normal for infants, it gradually diminishes and gets better at about five or six months when the child can discern that he is a separate entity from his mother. Until now he thought they were one physical unit that encompassed both mother and child. The minute he cried, his mother responded to his needs unconditionally. At age six months, it is no longer necessary to jump to fulfill the child's needs. The child is able to comprehend that his mother will feed him and take care of him even if it takes a few minutes of waiting. At age nine months, when the mother leaves the room, the baby no longer panics that he is being abandoned. He has the cognitive and mental skills to know that his mother will return.

But some parents continue to treat a four-year-old as if he were four months old, giving in to his demands immediately all the time. This child has never learned to move into the next stage of life, where gratification can wait a short while. The untrained child will balk at any parental attempt to forestall gratification by nagging, holding tantrums, or acting out. It is often so much easier for mothers to give in rather than take the pains to wean the child out of infant emotional behavior.

If you identify with such a situation, all is not lost. You can still bring your child into the next stage of development. While it is difficult and trying, the efforts are well worth the gains of your child's emotional growth. Three points that are extremely helpful in getting children unstuck from the patterns of the infant stage are consistency, limits, and consequences.

Consistency

Keep your promises of reward as well as your threats of punishment under all circumstances. Never should you neglect to keep your word. If this is difficult to carry through, then think twice before stating any promise or threat. Once a promise or threat has been made, only Mashiach can change it. Children need to believe in their parents. Regardless of how much love you give a child, he needs consistency just as much.

Giving love without consistency is like raising a child in a lopsided manner. It is like changing the recipe of a cake. Putting four cups of sugar and no flour into a cake will create a flop. The cake will have no consistency and be too sweet to enjoy. Parents cannot choose which mode of child-raising to embrace and which to ignore, just like we must keep all the commandments of the Torah, not pick and choose the ones we like.

Consistency instills confidence and security about the world via the parents, who represent the adult world. Not being consistent with a child sends the message that he cannot rely on his parents to protect him in the huge scary world of adulthood. When parents are weak in this area, children know that any promise made must be gratified immediately because they are not certain it will be done later. The message parents give is, "You'd better take it now because I'm not sure what mood I'll be in later."

Limits and Consequences

Children need limits. And if they overstep the bounds their parents have set, they must be made to suffer the consequences. This is as essential as food and water. When a child knows that parents will not punish him regardless of how serious the threat may be, he loses trust in his parents.

When a child has too many choices and liberties without enough consequences for negative actions, he becomes afraid of his own power. A young child does not have the maturity to manage his life no matter how high his IQ. Brains have little to do with emotions. All children need the security of knowing that someone bigger and stronger than them is making the ultimate disciplinary decisions. As much as they may protest, they need to feel that they cannot get away with not submitting to parental authority.

Parents who lack the ability to follow up on the consequences of negative behavior are sending the message "We are not dependable. You need to take care of yourself in this huge adult world. We cannot guide you and provide you with security to know that we are the caretakers and you are the child we take care of."

Another negative attribute children may adopt when they are not set limits is the ability to postpone gratification for a later time. They grow into young adults who need to have their impulses met *now*. This attitude is dangerous, especially from a Torah point of view. Most mitzvos in the Torah, such as not eating dairy after meat, not opening a light till after Shabbos, and davening at certain times of the day, cannot be done if instant gratification rules a person's emotional state. Carrying through with a punishment and setting limits is hardly a choice; it is a must if the child is to remain religious when he grows into adulthood.

For parents to be effective in instilling security, delaying gratification, and promoting emotional maturity, these three issues — consistency, limits, and follow up — need to be incorporated on a permanent basis. Do not feel guilty or afraid to set limits and give appropriate consequences and create a secure structure. Your child may balk when you are firm about these child-raising techniques. Do not panic. Remember that his message may be different from the content of his words. "I don't want to listen" may just be a test. It is like a fire drill to see how fire-proof, safe, and secure the environment of the home is.

Who Has the Problem?

THE VOICE on the phone sounded desperate. "Please, you must help me. The preschool my four-year-old is attending claims she is emotionally disturbed and retarded. They refuse to take her back for the coming year. She is now registered at the Bye Why Program, a school for the emotionally and mentally impaired."

The call is not unusual for the ODA Department of Social Services, where I work. We receive such calls on a daily basis, people pleading with social workers to do an immediate evaluation of a child about to be dumped into the category of "disabled" or "disturbed."

During the evaluation with Baila, the social workers saw no evidence of retardation or emotional illness. What they did see was a child who had been excessively exposed to poor role modeling.

The mother, a large, intimidating woman, insisted that no one liked her daughter, just as her neighbors didn't like her. They always huddled in groups whispering about her whenever she came out of her apartment. With anger and tears, she burst out, "Just because I am Israeli doesn't mean I am no good. Why do people always pick on me?"

Her suspicious and angry tone contrasted by her deep

sensitivity and pain signaled her own insecurities and
fears about adjusting to a new country with little or no
family support. Giving mixed messages of wanting to be
accepted yet being suspicious of anyone who was not Israeli, she confused her many neighbors who had, in fact,
tried many times to approach her but were met with
rejection.

Her four-year-old, Baila, quickly adopted the negative
messages that she was different and that the other kids in
the class were picking on her. Believing that outsiders beyond her nuclear family could not be trusted, she realized
early on that she had to take care of herself, regardless of
the consequences.

It was no wonder that the little girl refused to cooperate
when the teacher told her to clean up. She would bawl,
throw a fit, and shriek that the teacher was picking on her
to do the heavy work. When a child had a toy she wanted,
she grabbed it out of the child's hand and hid under the table with it. Any attempt from the teacher to coax her out
from under the table, give the toy back, or ask for it po-
litely was met with new bouts of shrieks and a physical
blow to the teacher's face while the unreasonable, angry
child screamed, "You hate me! You hate me! You are always picking on me!"

Baila would continue with her unreasonable behavior
throughout the day. She didn't participate in davening,
refused to make *berachos*, didn't recognize a single letter
of the alef-beis, and hit everyone within her reach. No
wonder the teachers, exasperated from their fruitless attempts to integrate her into the normal routine of the
class, eventually gave up on her. Just as mother and child
predicted, no one wanted to be her friend, and children

ran from her. Baila was stuck in a cycle of wanting friends but not knowing how to relate to them. Her teachers labeled her "unable to learn and play with others in a normal manner." This left the principal with no choice but to recommend a small classroom that catered to the needs of mentally and emotionally disturbed children.

It was at this point that the mother called the ODA social workers to evaluate her child. Much to the surprise of the principal, teachers, and mother, the social workers found Baila to be of superior intelligence that was being blocked by her inability to relate to others. Her violent bouts of anger resembled the impatient intolerance of a twelve-month-old rather than the mature tolerance of a child of four. Her communication with her teachers and classmates was so primitive, it mimicked symptoms of emotional disturbances coupled with retardation.

The social worker immediately advocated for the child to be given at least a three-month probationary period, during which time she would receive play therapy twice a week. Reluctantly, the principal relented.

At the beginning, when the concept of play therapy was explained to Baila, she refused to believe it. For forty-five minutes a week she was allowed to do as she wished — either play with any of the displayed toys or just sit and do nothing. During play therapy, Baila could do no wrong. Whatever she chose to do was validated and accepted unconditionally.

She didn't trust the system. At home her mother always told her what to do and what not to do. Suddenly she found herself having to make her own decisions unaided by her mother or teachers. She was lost. She would whine, "Tell me what to do. Tell me what to do."

After several unsuccessful attempts for direction, she began to make tiny decisions. Cautiously, full of fear, she would take the Magic Markers, but she was unsure which colors to use. Baila hoped I would say, "Use the red," so she could respond, "No, I hate the red! I don't want the red! I hate the red, and I hate you, too!" Her learned behavior was to respond in a negative manner just the way her mother did when neighbors tried to befriend her.

Being under the control of a teacher allowed her the opportunity to copy her mother's behavior. Play therapy threw her off because no demands were made on her — she was the initiator, the one in control. She had never experienced such freedom before and did not know how to use it.

No wonder Baila trembled the first time she made a decision to make a picture of a house with a green marker all on her own. Next she drew a picture of a mommy in the house. The mother was so big, her head stuck out of the roof of the house, colliding with the chimney. The father was not home. She explained that he was at work. Next she drew a picture of a little girl so small I had to lean forward to catch her features. She had sad-looking eyes and a blank look.

It was obvious to us that she felt small and unimportant, while her mother's need dominated the entire house. For the first time, I really felt that she would be betraying her mother if she didn't "feel along." In the process of such intense empathy, she never developed her own personality, views, and taste. Being a good girl meant being like Mommy and believing that her teachers and classmates were all out to get her, as if she was branded.

As play therapy progressed, Baila ever so slowly began

to realize that she was a separate identity from her mother. The enmeshment had dissolved. Now she was ready to find out who she was and what her personality was like.

Within a few short months, we discovered a sweet child who loved the color green, hated the color black, liked to play house, but hated to paint. She also let us know that she liked some children, while others she could ignore during playtime in school. She also discovered that she had a beautiful voice and began to sing the songs she learned in school. One day she said, "My mother hates when I sing, so I sing when I'm in the bathroom."

Finally, Baila was able to differentiate her personality from her mother's. As a result, she allowed herself to enjoy the activities at school and began to pick up the letters of the alef-beis quicker than most children. She no longer had to rebel to ally with Mom, so her real self, which was bright, articulate, and personable, emerged.

When her mother heard that her daughter was improving in school, she was thrilled. She had finally done something right in this strange country. Her daughter had become a success in school, and the mother began to admit that the teachers did indeed like her daughter. If her daughter was likeable, then perhaps she was, too.

Cautiously she began to accept "hellos" and respond warmly to her neighbors instead of shutting the door. Soon a neighbor stopped by Friday night to ask if Baila could come to play with her daughter. The mother readily agreed, and while Baila ran next door, the neighbor stayed until the men came home from shul. Today, a year later, both mother and daughter are doing well socially.

This true story is a typical example of how a child's disturbances may be a reflection of the mother's internal struggles. Both mother and child may not even be aware that this "personality imitation" is happening. A child often follows the mood and personality of a mother, not knowing that it could be any other way. The mother may be involved with the multifaceted job of being teacher, tutor, doctor, lawyer, judge, social worker, cook, and doing enough loads of laundry to compete with the Chinese laundry down the block. It is difficult to remain cool, calm, and collected at all times. It is even more difficult when personal adult pressures threaten to spill over, breaking the safety of the family structure.

It takes more than strength of mind for a mother to contain herself when faced with an emotional dilemma; she must have strength of personality as well. Parents need to realize that children feel their anxieties and often experience them automatically and with the same intensity as they do.

Most children will face some sort of confusion and dilemma at some stage of their emotional development. Let us be prepared to correct and control an emotional dilemma before it disrupts the child's stability.

3 to 6 Years

Initiative versus Guilt

This stage requires a repertoire of motor, mental, and social growth through outlets of free play and outdoor activities. Children who are given ample opportunities to "practice for adult life" through play, fun, and games develop initiative, enthusiasm, and skills for adult challenges both academically and socially.

Children who are pushed into adult responsibilities, such as a serious school environment, before having adequate time to develop their skills through play may become passive recipients, inhibiting optimal emotional growth.

It is a happy talent to know how to play.

— Ralph Waldo Emerson

Preschool:
A Sensitive Issue

During the preschool years, a child continues to expand his horizon of mental comprehension and socialization. Now he can better understand the term *sharing* and can play in a give-and-take manner. This stage of life is most significant in that the child is provided with many opportunities to play at length and prepare himself for the adult world. Through play he gains the social maturity of communication, gains a sense of identity, and rehearses adult roles. The more a child practices play skills, the more he gains the social and cognitive skills to meet the challenges of adulthood. The major decision parents make for preschool children is whether or not to begin formal learning.

Preschool as an Advantage

Preschool is a blessing for the mother who has two or three preschoolers at home. Sending the three-, four-, and five-year-old to school frees the mother from being the caretaker all day and provides respite and time for household duties. The child, too, loves the company of friends, improves his social skills, and gains from the stimulating environment.

As an added bonus, the child comes home with an education. He learns reading, knowledge of religious customs, biblical stories, and arts and crafts, which delight the mother, grandparents, and relatives. Also, if a three- or four-year-old is not sent to school, this often means not having any friends on the block to play with. When the child enters school a year later than his friends, he may face the disadvantage of not being up to par academically with his peers.

Preschool as a Disadvantage

When preschool concentrates more on formal learning than play, the experience becomes more detrimental than advantageous. Many schools, in their zeal to show off due to competition with other schools, limit playtime and focus on formal academic learning. Skipping play can create lifelong disadvantages to the preschooler that cannot be overemphasized.

The average preschool-age child has not yet developed the mental skills necessary to put sounds and letters together. Mastering written language requires lots of repetition, long hours of concentration, and the physical maturity to sit for long periods of time. Most preschoolers cannot conform to such strict mental and physical demands. They become anxious, pressured, and often turned off of learning altogether. In their struggles to please the teacher and parent, they sacrifice their need for informal play, which is vastly more valuable to their long-term emotional and mental stability.

The most ideal preschool setting is one that allows ample time for the child to play and does not jump on the bandwagon to produce mini-geniuses. By encouraging individual and group play, the children overcome imaginary fears, mold their self-image, and develop the motor and mental development necessary for formal learning. Not only do these children enjoy learning later in life, but they also gain the emotional and social maturity to interact with others in the present and future. Zigler sums it up well:

> Our four-year-olds have a place in school, but it is not at a school desk.

It's Not What You Teach but How You Teach

Boys in general begin formal education at an earlier age than girls do. It is essential for the teacher of little boys to understand that their cognitive, emotional, and physical development is not any more mature than girls of the same age. What, then, should a rebbe or teacher do? They are caught between two views: to instill Torah values and davening at an early age or to wait for every child to be ready despite the pressures of the parents and school administration.

In such a situation, the best approach is to use creativity, songs, games, and play in the lessons. Instead of expecting the child to conform to mature measures, such as sitting for long periods of time, being punished for not knowing an answer, or repeated drilling, the teacher should conform to the maturity level of the children. The learning should be in the form of play. In this manner, the child learns Torah values and reading, but his need to socialize, play, and have fun is not compromised.

Turning Learning into Play

Many more teachers would teach through play if they

were aware of the detrimental consequences premature formal learning can have on the child for life. Yes, it does take more effort, more preparation, and patience, but the results are well worth the effort. Preschool children who are taught through play learn to love learning. Children who are taught most of the day at the desk can become burned out before they even enter first grade.

Parents need to take an active role in the education of the preschool child. Is the alef-beis being taught through songs and preschool-level activities? Is the parashah an enjoyable forum in which children are actively involved, acting out the characters and story scenes of the parashah (costumes, putting on plays for the class, and songs are valuable tools), or are they sitting behind a desk being pressured to concentrate?

The question that has to be raised isn't so much what is being taught, but rather how it is taught. If the learning agenda can be turned into play, great. If it cannot be turned into play, don't teach it. The short-term gains of *nachas* from showing off little geniuses today are not worth the long-term consequences to the child at a later age.

FOUR-YEAR-OLD EFRAIM was in a kindergarten class with a highly motivated teacher. The kindergarten had toys and games, but they were rarely used, since the teacher spent most of the day teaching alef-beis and ABCs and making masterpieces with the children with arts and crafts.

One day, little Efraim, out of the blue, blurted out, "I want to get married. I want to get married, and I want to do it right away. I don't care if I have to marry my little sister Faige, even though she fights with me all day."

The teacher was taken aback by the unusual statement. Trying to contain herself, she asked, "Why do you want to get married, Efraim?"

Efraim did not take long to reply. He had his answer prepared since the first day of school, when he spent forty minutes sitting in a circle, learning three topics. "I asked Mommy how much longer I will have to go to school, and she said, until I get married."

How to Teach Morality to the Growing Child

By the time the average child has reached first grade, he has spent much time observing the behavior of his parents, teachers, and other significant adults. If the preaching of adults has been consistent with their behavior, children have little or no problem in following suit. If the mother or teachers give contradictory messages to children about morality, children become confused and lose respect for the lesson.

Before a child can fully internalize the goodness or badness of a particular act, he must witness consistency of instruction with practice. A mother tells a child not to lie. Later she screams from the basement to the child, who has just picked up the phone, "I'm doing laundry. Tell her I'm not home." She is doing more damage to the child's morality than she would to the household chore that is difficult to interrupt. A load of dirty laundry can be washed later, but a child's perception of honesty may have become corrupted forever.

Teachers who tell students that learning Torah is wonderful since it teaches human beings how to treat one another must not contradict their statements by hurting the feelings of their students. This contradiction between teaching and performance can cause long-term anxiety, confusion, and emotional damage to the child's present and future religious conduct. When children are taught respectfully, they are better equipped to approach others with respect.

Molding a Child's Personality and Character

At six, the child already has a conscience of his own and can feel guilty over having done an incorrect act, such as hitting or eating before washing. Even when not in the presence of a parent or teacher, the six-year-old will most often behave in the same manner as he does in public.

However, parents should not rely solely on the fact that they love their child to teach morality. Such instincts are not inborn. They have to be taught, disciplined, shaped, and molded over and over as the child's cognitive ability changes with age. To be effective, parents must convey intensity, seriousness, consistency with negative and positive reinforcement, and respect to the child at each stage of his emotional development.

The child who has been taught early on appropriate behaviors and has observed his parents and teachers "practicing what they preach" is most likely to integrate these patterns of life into everyday living. Clary and Miller are concerned about the effects of mixed messages children receive in response to altruism. They have found that adults who behaved in immoral ways tended to come from families in which altruism was limited to preaching and where the ideals were often violated in practice. These young people, angered by the discrepancy between parental actions, had undergone a crisis of hypocrisy during childhood. The result was the inability to make or remain consistent with their own commitments to morality.

Attitudes

Attitudes are just as important as behaviors. A mother who is anxious for weeks, if not months, about cleaning for Pesach and complains about the difficulties instead of explaining the miracles God performed for the Jews during their departure from Egypt will find that her children will adopt her negative attitude.

> ONE FOUR-YEAR-OLD who did not fully comprehend the concept of Pesach kept hearing his mother shout, "Stop going into that room with food. Pesach is coming. Don't eat that now. Pesach is just around the corner."
>
> One day, the four-year-old shouted back with a sincere flare of anger, "When Pesach gets here, I will beat him up for making Mommy work so hard."

An adult who fondly remembers her mother sharing the joys of challah baking by allowing her as a young child to play with some of the dough will most likely enjoy baking challos for her own family. For a child to enjoy religious rituals, he needs a role model who enjoys them.

The most important features to take into account when raising emotionally healthy children who will follow the religious patterns of their parents are actively teaching why a behavior is appropriate or inappropriate, negative and positive reinforcement, setting an example, and sharing positive attitudes in performing religious rituals.

Play Therapy

I'm at a wedding, relishing the thought of a four-course meal after a hectic week of living off yogurt, farmer cheese, and crackers when someone taps me on the shoulder.

"I hope you don't mind." Her voice sounds desperate. "I hear you do play therapy with children. I have a five-year-old son who wets himself. It has gotten so bad, the school sends him home."

I wish I could tell her that I'm famished and that I do mind being interrupted but don't. I understand her immense frustration and sudden relief in finding someone who has worked with hundreds of children who wet. I push my plate aside, trying to drown my hunger pangs with ice water, and listen.

Sometimes it's at a *shiur*. I gratefully slump into a seat ready to be a passive listener for a change when I notice a heavyset woman whom I had grown up with waving her hands toward me frantically. "Save me a seat. I must talk to you."

She arrives huffing. Beads of perspiration begin to form a trickle as she gasps, not even giving herself enough time to catch her breath, "Remember when I told you I had twins?"

Without waiting for a reply she pants on, "One of the twins is stuttering. It gets worse each time his twin brother, who is bigger than he is, hits him over the head. What should I do? Is it emotional? It is neurological?" The speaker is being introduced, and I can't hear a word. "Do you think you can give him an evaluation tomorrow morning? I'll keep him home from school if I have to."

I am filled with mixed emotions. I came to hear the *shiur* to get away from work and to gain a bit of *chizuk*, not to discuss play therapy. On the other hand, I feel the deep dilemma of the woman who waited ten years for the gift of two bundles of joy, only to realize that with the joy comes hard work, aggravation, and problems. I whisper to her softly that I will speak to her during intermission. She reminds me loudly that there is no intermission; this is not a school play. The lady behind us gives a loud *sshhhh*, and I quickly promise to stay a few minutes after the *shiur*.

What is play therapy all about? First, we must realize that the help does not come from the social worker such as my friend Sara Freund and myself. It comes directly from Hashem. We are only His privileged agents given the holy gift of fulfilling his task in helping children heal.

Play therapy does little to help children who suffer from severe neurological or mental disorders such as autism, retardation, or schizophrenia. It helps mostly normal children who need to deal with a change in their lives, such as moving, a new sibling, or a new school. It is wonderful in extracting the effects of trauma, building low self-esteem, and giving concrete instructions and support to parents on raising difficult children. It does not cure attention deficit disorder, ADHD, or learning disabilities. It does, however, help the therapist recognize misdiagnosed children labeled with these disorders. It helps with stuttering if it is not caused by a speech impairment and helps children control antisocial behaviors such as stealing, violent outbursts, and impulse control. It also lifts anxiety, depression, and failure to thrive in a school setting.

People often ask, "Which problem is play therapy most likely to heal?" My answer is always the same: "The ones parents are willing to face and work at with the therapist as a team, coming consistently for a set period of time."

Children often have a difficult time articulating what bothers them. What they claim is bothering them, such as a stomachache, may be a symptom of a real problem such as school phobia. When should a mother run to the doctor rather than the therapist? The rule of thumb is to always check with a competent pediatrician for a physical cause for pain before assuming the pain is emotional. When this has been done and the child continues to complain that school gives him a stomachache, you may still be in the forest. What is it about school that makes him so anxious? If you ask your child this question, you will probably receive answers like "I don't know," "No one likes me in school," "I hate the school lunch," "I do like school, but the teacher looks funny," or "I want to go to another school."

Parents are baffled and rightfully so. Time goes on. Mother tries to reassure the child, but still the stomachaches continue. Father bribes the child to go by offering to buy him a new bike. Child smiles and agrees. A week after the shiny bike is bought the child no longer has stomachaches. He now begins to wet his bed during the night three years after having been trained. Mother ignores it. Father yells at him for being too lazy to get up in the middle of the night. Shlomie is given the task of reminding Chaim to use the bathroom before bedtime. Suri begins to make fun of him and calls him a baby. By this time,

Chaim begins to wet during the day as well. The school asks the mother to send an extra set of clean clothes each day. Bubby says its because he started school too early. Zeidy says, "Just give him two *petch* and everything will be fine."

In the course of play therapy, we see a normal child who has a buildup of insecurities, fears, low self-esteem, and rage. We do therapy via toys, games, arts and crafts, painting, and talking. The therapy is not the toy, the doll, or the game. It's what he does with the objects in the room, how he utilizes the toys, the message he writes on the blackboard, the meaning of his puppet show, the crafts he creates with the hammer, wood, and magnet that tell the story of the heart. How he plays and the manner in which he expresses himself tell us more than words can say. The equipment of the playroom serves as the vehicle to express internal pain.

One child may use paint to express his trauma of being lost in the supermarket and having the manager page his mother. Another child may use the doll house to accurately play out his feeling of being ignored by his parents. Still another child will bang for half an hour with tools to let us know how frustrated he feels toward his rebbe or father who expect more of him than he can perform academically.

Then there is the child who refuses to do anything. She shuts down and rebels by doing nothing. Much to her surprise, we can easily pick up her need for control. Maybe she has too many tasks at home and feels guilty for resenting them. Here in the play therapy forum she can express her needs with or without words and begin to understand her real issues. Once the issues are understood and resolved, symptoms such as school phobia, wetting, acting out, and apathy begin to dissipate. The resolved issue takes away the need for the symptom.

When play therapy was administered to Chaim, the real issue was addressed rather than the symptom of wetting. As a result, Chaim found it less necessary to use a secondary outlet for his frustration. As time went on, the bed wetting decreased, and the child stopped complaining about school.

The therapist plays an intricate part in the drama of play therapy. Her main role is to create a climate where the child feels totally safe to be his authentic self. This is done by accepting the child for what he is without ifs and buts. Unconditional regard and respect is given to the child regardless of what he does or does not do. If he wants to do an Indian dance, that is accepted as much as the child who just wants to sit and do nothing. Once the pressure to perform is off, the child slowly begins to do and be who he wants to be, not what society is pressuring him to be.

Chaim demonstrated via a puppet show his hate for the bully who stole his snack and *tzedakah* money on a daily basis. Little Chaim may have been threatened and too frightened to tell his mother the real reason he feared school. This caused his morning stomachaches. Ten shiny bikes could not alleviate Chaim's fear. Play therapy did. It helped him express the reason he hated school. Further intervention with the parents, school, and more therapy rebuilt his bruised self-confidence, and he learned to protect his ego and property.

This true story is typical of what I see in my work. Again and again, it amazes me how devoted parents find themselves baffled about a particular child's behavior. Often the closer a person is to the pain of his loved one, the harder it is for him to be of concrete help. Even the best of parents are only human and may need to reach out to professionals for emotional detective work.

Confidence is instilled by the therapist who validates every move and action of the child in the play therapy room. Validation and reflection gives the constant message "You're okay." Later the message changes to "You're special, strong, and capable." This encouragement motivates the child to further express his internal frustrations using the tools of the play therapy room, which translates into a forum to ventilate emotions, master the problem, and gain self-esteem from the experience of success. The gains snowball. With continued help from Hashem, the child becomes transformed from a whining, unhappy child to one of poise and confidence, ready to face the challenges of school and home.

These early successes will be the stepping stones to the foundation of an emotionally healthy adult performing at his optimal innate self. If he is sitting and learning in *kollel*, he will do so diligently and happily. If he is in business, he will have the confidence to stand up to work pressures. If he chooses to be a rebbe, he will be a master at motivating children to love learning without having to resort to copious punishment. Before an adult can be a happy, productive human being serving Hashem, he must first have been a happy productive child. One cannot skip over chronic childhood issues. And the child will not grow out of them. They may recede temporarily, waiting for adulthood to burst forth in full force.

Whose Phobia Is It Anyway?

MRS. BROWN brought her little Breina to us for an evaluation. The child seemed to have school phobia. Until six years of age she had been a normal child, happy, friendly, sociable, and bright. Her incoming neuroses were the symptoms she manifested toward her hatred of school.

Each morning she would throw herself on the floor and scream loud enough to wake up the dead. The baby in the next room would immediately join in the wailing, while elderly Mrs. Gross, who lived directly below the Browns, would bang on her ceiling to signal her annoyance at the noise. But her efforts were in vain. The only one to hear was her Italian neighbor whose dog barked louder than Breina.

Still, Breina would not stop the screaming, not until two things happened. One day, someone in the building called the police. When they arrived, they could not trace the origin of the racket. They knocked on all thirty-two doors of the apartment building. When everyone had congregated into the airless hall, the screams stopped. Breina was also curious — she thought someone was being robbed early in the morning.

There was a second, less dramatic episode but more frightening. Breina no longer wanted to say Shema at night. She softly admitted that she did not want Hashem to return her *neshamah* anymore. She would rather go to Gan Eden than back to school even for one more day.

Mrs. Brown called the Learning Center, desperate for an emergency evaluation. She had read our article on school burnout in a periodical and hoped we could help her little Breina. Perhaps Breina was reacting to the extreme pressures of first grade.

The results of the evaluation were puzzling. Breina demonstrated no pathology. She was friendly, allowed her mother to wait in the waiting room without a fuss, ruling out the possibly of some kind of separation anxiety, and started to play almost immediately. The more I scrutinized her responses to new adults and environmental stimuli, interpreted her colorful pictures, and followed her actively from game to creative arts and crafts, the more I was convinced that this child was absolutely healthy. I almost did not believe that she created the racket her mother had described. The child with morning depression clearly did not match the articulate six-year-old who excitedly beat me at checkers and demanded a prize for each game she won.

The evaluation was almost over, leaving me clueless, when I noticed she was staring at the blackboard. I mentioned that we had colored chalk to use if she wished. Like a sudden thunderstorm, her face clouded, and a shower of tears sprang from her eyes as she fell to the floor in a spastic seizure. The only difference between her seizure and an epileptic one was that she was totally in control. She seemed to know exactly what she was doing. She was yelling, "I hate school! I'm not going back to school ever," she ranted. Her shoe loosened as she kicked, and it flew across the room, hitting the blackboard with a great thrust.

Breina was taken by surprise. She forgot her tantrum. She sat up, stunned for a moment, and then laughter mingled with the wet tears as she struggled to articulate her emotions. "I paid you back. I paid you back," she repeated over and over with newfound feelings of revenge that had replaced her inner turmoil of anger. I wondered who she was punishing but did not interrupt her spontaneous expression of emotion.

Suddenly Breina got up from the floor. She wobbled to the doll house and said she wanted to play school. A lady became the bad teacher whom she immediately began hitting. When that wasn't enough, she took the wooden doll and banged its head against the wall, screaming, "Mommy hates you! Mommy hates you! Why did you blame Mommy? Why did you shame Mommy?"

Breina was expressing retaliation, revenge, and hate, but the source of these intense emotions was not clear. I did not rule out the possibility of school trauma, but I also wondered if the feelings belonged to her at all or whether it was someone else's anxieties she felt compelled to express. I wondered if her mother hadn't subconsciously projected some of her own anxieties about school onto her daughter. Had the mother been traumatized in school and had never resolved her own issues? It's not uncommon for parents to transmit their opinions, attitudes, neuroses, and even phobias onto their children. Most often this is done innocently with neither parent nor child being aware of it.

Suddenly ten-year-old Yankel, who had been a client years ago, came to my mind. Yankel was so afraid of the dark that a 120-watt bulb had to burn in his room all night or he would get nightmares. He never ventured outside at night. In the country, when his bunk organized a campfire, he went only after being equipped with a portable phone and a handyman's commercial flashlight. While his mother wept and complained about how Yankel's night phobia affected her lifestyle, since he didn't permit her to leave the house at night either unless she, too, carried a phone and flashlight, his father mentioned that he wasn't surprised at all. His mother-in-law often complained that she had never been able to go to *simchahs* unless she took her little girl along.

Immediately Yankel's mother began to cry. "Everyone knows why I was afraid of the dark and still am," she sobbed. "When I was a little girl, a man once pulled me into his car on a summer night. He stuffed my mouth with a rag so my screams couldn't be heard. Luckily my friends saw and alerted my mother, who quickly called the police. The story ended with no major injury other than a fear of the dark."

Empathetically I asked how she had gotten over her phobia. She admitted that she hadn't. "Whenever I have to go out, I take a Valium, and that calms me."

It was clear then that somehow Yankel had inherited his mother's internal anxiety toward dark and adopted the phobia as if the trauma had occurred to him. In all likelihood, the mother was totally innocent. She probably never even told the story to Yankel or verbally expressed her fear of the dark. Still, children have sensitive antennas that can pick up on unexpressed emotions. Without realizing it, they take on parental fears as if they are their own. They do not have the ego strength to separate their fragile identities from those of their parents. Emotions, attitudes, and feelings (positive as well as negative) that are internally felt by parents are often felt by the child as well.

I wondered if here, too, there had been a transmission of phobia from mother to child. When Mrs. Brown came in, my first question was whether she had suffered some trauma in school. She was shocked at my brazen question. She had brought Breina in because of the child's school phobia. Why was I asking questions about Mrs. Brown's own school experiences? She was a bit apprehensive, if not offended, but answered nevertheless. She had never liked school but never protested the way Breina did. She had known she was expected to go to school.

I probed on. When did Breina begin to hate school?

It was clear that Breina had not protested going to preschool. Her tantrums began this year in first grade. Mrs. Brown found this difficult to handle, since she had always been an outsider, being an immigrant from Hungary who spoke only Hungarian for the first ten years of her life. Not knowing any English or Hebrew, the shy ten-year-old was placed in the first grade with six-year-olds who made fun of her. Since she was tall for her age, they had called her "Empire State Building." Though too naive to understand what the Empire State Building was, she had realized she was being ridiculed.

When she finally did learn English, it was with a thick

accent that made the girls in class giggle. To gain attention and recognition, she became a troublemaker. Girls accepted her when she volunteered to be the one to put gum on the teacher's chair or agreed to steal the test from the teacher's bag the day before it was to be given and to make a photocopy of it. She never even tried to study for her tests. She accepted her low grades like one receives junk mail. She would crumple up the test papers and throw them in the wastebasket without another glance.

I probed for a specific trauma. What happened to Mrs. Brown in grade school that could have possibly been transmitted to little Breina? Mrs. Brown thought and thought. "On the contrary," she insisted, shaking her head, "today I am a teacher myself. I always tell the children that there is hope for everyone. I teach fourth grade, and I'm embarrassed at my daughter's daily reaction to school, especially since we are both in the same school."

I'd often thought being a social worker was an umbrella job that included detective work, and today I was convinced. Unable to solve the mystery, I advised Mrs. Brown to be firm and empathic while she readied her daughter for school. Breina should also be brought for play therapy twice a week to allow her the opportunity to express her fears, learn anger management skills, resolve her pain, and, most important, gain an understanding of the origin of her phobia.

Play therapy did help her cope with her situation, but it was her mother who finally found the origin of her deep phobia. She remembered that during the past summer Breina had once stayed home from day camp due to a common cold. As usual, a clan of ladies would sit under the tree and relax until lunchtime exchanging stories and tidbits on the topic of child-raising.

Breina, sitting snugly in Mommy's lap, seemed undisturbed as Mrs. Brown was sharing her own trauma that happened to her in first grade when she was ten years old, the Empire State Building of the class. The girl sitting in front of her had an accident, making a splattering noise in the quiet class. All eyes turned toward the direction of the dripping sound. The classroom's wooden floor was not properly leveled, and the stream trailed toward Miriam, forming a puddle beneath her desk. The class burst into fits of uncontrollable laughter.

The teacher was furious at the young girl's lack of bladder control. She made poor Miriam stand up on her desk as the entire class was directed to point their finger at the giant Empire State Building and shout, "Shame, shame, baby! Shame, shame, baby!" The poor girl tried to protest but to no avail. She only made things worse. Her Hungarian protests infuriated the teacher and made the children giggle louder than ever. Order was finally restored when she wiped the floor clean with paper towels and was then sent to the corner.

While the class returned to normal, Mrs. Brown's attitude became extremely hostile and angry. She carried the experience every day of her life as an unresolved first-grade trauma. While she coped with it the best she could, rebelling but eventually settling down, her little Breina, who had heard the story four weeks before she started first grade, took over the responsibility of revenge mixed with anger, fear, and hatred.

No wonder she refused to enter first grade with excitement and anticipation. Doing so would be betraying her mother's agony, which she had taken as her own. The yoke of resentment became hers. To add fuel to the fire, having Breina about to enter first grade may have triggered Mrs. Brown's own anxieties over the episode, which were never addressed.

Which came first? Was the mother's personal horrendous experience in first grade triggered by Breina entering first grade, or was Breina's phobia a result of hearing her mother tell her tragic story to her friends? Even if Breina had not heard the story, would she have picked up her mother's anxieties about first grade?

These questions were never really answered, and I still wonder about it sometimes.

What was made clear from this experience is how parental attitudes and opinions affect our children. Both spoken and unspoken attitudes transmit messages more vividly than we would like to believe. In this case, Breina was lucky. She expressed her anguish so loudly that it demanded and received attention.

First, her mother explained the traumatic story to Breina and softly gave her permission to let go of the yoke of responsibility. Further play therapy helped her express her anxieties, and within two weeks, Breina was no longer throwing tantrums. Mrs. Gross stopped banging the ceiling, and the frightened dog stopped barking. Best of all, Mrs. Brown had decided that while Breina had recovered from her trauma, she herself would begin to resolve her own issues through therapy. She put it better than any professional: "It's time to stop the intergenerational traumas that affected me and my child. If I don't begin to work through the residue, I may still be unconsciously transmitting unhealthy anxieties to Breina and my other children. I want to be normal, and I want my children to be normal."

I quickly corrected her. "Your reactions are and were perfectly normal, Mrs. Brown. The episode that occurred was not normal. The fact that you are ready to face the trauma shows tremendous strength, maturity, and, most of all, emotional health."

6 to 11 Years

Industry versus Inferiority

During the elementary school years, the child thrives on learning concepts and figuring out how things operate. Academically he is enthused and prompted to perform according to the amount of validation and recognition he receives for his performance. A child who is praised and valued for his achievements will aim for greater heights.

Children who are ignored or invalidated lose enthusiasm and stagnate in their academic, emotional, and social growth.

We are molded and remolded by those who have loved us, and though the love may pass, we are nevertheless their work, for good or ill.

— Francois Mauriac

School Is Not Only for Children

A mother's involvement or noninvolvement in her children's schooling plays a large role in promoting emotionally healthy children. The issues that need to be examined are (a) what to expect from the school in terms of providing an academic and nurturing environment, (b) when to ignore a problem, allowing the child to work it out on his own, and (c) when to get involved by directly contacting the school or teacher.

Too Much Involvement

In general, most children have gained enough social skills to handle diverse personalities by the time they reach first grade. Parental intervention is necessary only when the imbalance of power makes it impossible for the child to solve his problem. This occurs when the teacher, the authority figure, makes demands that are not age appropriate and the child cannot defend himself due to his position as a student.

The parent is in a sensitive position. If she runs to rescue the child each time he has a problem, the child will never learn to fend for himself. In all probability, as an adult he will feel like a coward each time a difficulty occurs, such as in tenant-landlord relationships, monetary matters, and in-law differences. His self-esteem will be too weak or undeveloped to handle normal adult issues.

On the other side of the coin is the mother who strongly feels that children have to take care of all their school issues independently. She has her issues to handle, and the children have their issues to handle. Ironically, these children may very well grow up with the same low self-esteem as the children of the overconscientious mother. Always being in the wrong in school issues gives them a feeling of "learned helplessness." "Whatever I do, I will always be wrong." These feelings contribute to low self-esteem.

As adults, these children will not bother to fight for their rights because they know from childhood experience that they can never win anyway. In all probability they will allow their landlord, in-laws, and business associates to take advantage of them. They know and feel that "sticking up for myself won't help anyway, so I might as well not even waste my energy."

When to Get Involved

The rule of thumb is that if the complaints of the child interfere with his functioning at home and spill over into other areas of his life, parental intervention is warranted. This can occur in the following situations:

1. A child is attacked by another classmate, and his own attempts to stop the attacks have failed. In this situation, the mother can call the school, the teacher, or perhaps the mother of the child who is inflicting the attacks.

2. A teacher exhibits penalty behaviors that are detrimental to the physical or emotional welfare of the child. This may happen when a teacher is nervous by nature and lashes out at the children, either physically or verbally, as a first response to misconduct. If physical punishment is permitted by the school, it should be used with caution. Too much hitting will make the child feel as if he is living in a war zone and most certainly will erode his natural enthusiasm to learn. If physical punishment is an accepted form of reinforcement, it should never be used as a first alternative, but rather as a last resort. It is the responsibility of every parent to ensure that the learning environment is a nurturing one that provides appropriate consequences for misconduct.

3. A teacher who has low self-esteem needs to prove herself by overteaching. Perhaps due to school pressure or inexperience, teachers may pressure children with too much school work and homework, leaving little time for the child to formulate friendships and enjoyable activities. Taking away a child's free time and replacing it with more school work can create a talking, walking human encyclopedia masking an emotionally crippled child. Many school-age geniuses suffer from involuntary jerking motions, bed wetting, depression, and anxieties.

In such situations, the parent must intervene to find out if the source of the problem is that her child cannot keep up or the teacher is outpacing the capabilities of the average child. A clear understanding must be established, with respectful communication. A mother's intervention is vital to the long-term academic and emotional growth of the child.

Finding the balance of when to reach out and when to stay out should be the goal of concerned parents. The best way to reach the middle ground is to have an open, objective view of both the school and the personality of the child. If the negative circumstances are not personality related, but school related, mothers can make a big difference. It takes a confident mother to take action. The result of her efforts will be an adjusted student functioning at optimal level.

School Burnout:
Who's to Blame?

The school blames the parents, the parents blame the school, and the ones getting hurt while the argument rages on are our own schoolchildren. Most children are born within the average range of intelligence that develop at age-appropriate intervals. Social and emotional maturity develops very much like intelligence, at normal stages of child development. No amount of multivitamins, vigorous drilling, or medication can speed the intelligent, social, and emotional growth of children. What aggressive intervention does do successfully is dull their enthusiasm for learning before formal school has even begun.

A few decades ago, school began at six years of age. The children were taught the Hebrew and English alphabet, then progressed to reading and writing. By the end of first grade, most students knew how to daven and read first-grade-level readers. Between subjects, the class played games and had fun with the teacher.

Today most children start nursery at about three years of age. This is okay if the academics is held off until the preschooler reaches first grade and the preschool child engages in individual play, socializes with peers, interacts in group play via indoor games, and gets outside physical stimulation. All the while, teachers should shower the youngsters with tons of love, validation for achievements, and individual attention.

Unfortunately such healthy preschool scenes are almost obsolete and sound like a fairy tale. They have been replaced by preschools competing to produce mini-geniuses at the tender ages of three, four, and five. Instead of concentrating on innovative ways to promote enthusiasm for learning through songs, plays, and games that center around religious subjects, they emphasize group projects, group drilling of letters, and page-long parashah questions to prove the competence of the teacher.

And the teachers succeed. They bask in the glory of being able to teach four-year-olds math, both the Hebrew and English alphabet, and even davening, while social and interpersonal skills are ignored. Attention and validation are rewarded to the child who brings the "*nachas* sheets" back stamped with the parents' signature of approval.

The children who can comply with such expectations are the gifted children — and every class has some. The rest of the class feels pressured, inadequate, and stupid. As for the successful students, the price they pay for knowing the "*Mah Nishtanah*" in Hebrew, Yiddish, and English is too high. In the end, no child in the class really benefits from such formal structure regardless of how impressive he may appear. While the teachers beam with pride and parents *shep nachas*, the children are being robbed — yes, robbed — of their only chance to learn lifelong living skills and practice for adulthood.

The reality is that there is no way a child can speed the

process of developing enthusiasm toward learning. It's a process that develops naturally if patience allows it. Unfortunately, the world is in a great rush. Our scholars enter first grade prematurely and are more than likely already burned out. Instead of excitement in discovering language, books, and reading, they groan, "Not again! We did that already. When is the fun going to start?"

Once upon a time, not too long ago, children used to look forward to homework, which began in first grade, marking a big milestone in their tender years. Today they no longer want to bother with it by the time they turn six. They have been choked with homework for a year or two already and balk at more.

Once upon a time, parents trusted schools to be the authority on education. They stayed out of the classroom, permitting the experts to determine the level of academia. Naturally the children emulated the respect and positive attitudes of their parents. Their faces glowed with excitement and curiosity when they entered first grade. Owning a first *sefer* or book was the most significant event in their lives. The thought of doing homework with brand-new, sharpened pencils made them feel six feet tall, and a notebook was proof that they had become responsible and ready to conquer the challenges of learning.

That was long ago. Today there is nothing exciting about first grade other than uniforms. Everything else was already drilled into them a hundred times, a hundred different ways, and now they have had enough.

No wonder they sit rigid in their seats, listless, unable to concentrate. Before long the teacher requests a conference with the parents advising them to get an evaluation for the possibility of ADHD or other learning disabilities.

Perhaps the ones to be evaluated are not the children, but the school systems that foster such unrealistic preschool curricula. Maybe the school director was a gifted academic genius who preferred books over playing house at age five. No wonder she cannot relate to the normal pre-scholar with average intelligence and an insatiable need to express himself through play. Perhaps the principal is addressing the needs of parents who demand higher education. Perhaps what the parents do not know is that while children today start school earlier than they did, their academic, social, and emotional maturity does not develop any faster. Years ago, as children, they themselves were not required to jump over the stage of play — the most essential need of preschoolers — and tune in to pressured, serious learning before they were ready; today's children are.

When pushing children to learn begins to demand its price, it is often devastating to the entire family. Mother feels like a failure, father reprimands the child to try harder, teachers shake their heads in despair, and the child curls up in shame and helplessness. Before long the parents begin to question the expectations of the school and blame them for creating the problem in the child. The school retaliates. They say that compared to every parent who wants to slow down the academic race, there are ten parents who feel children should be even better prepared for first grade. Not keeping up with the general learning level of other schools means low registration and a reputation for being a school for slow children. In frustration, they claim that the parents are in denial that their child has problems.

Who suffers from this unresolved cycle of blame? The children, of course. But we should not focus on who is to blame for this mess but rather on how parents and schools can clean it up.

Student Rivalry:
Can It Really Hurt?

S tudent rivalry goes back to one-room schoolhouses. It has always been an issue but never more than now. With over-crowded classes, it is difficult to oversee the politics of the students. Besides, the job of the teacher is to teach, not to serve as a policeman in the schoolyard. Yet some sort of intervention is necessary. Children cannot be trusted to channel their anger, competition, and emotions appropriately. Sometimes even normal children from good homes can become tyrants on the school bus toward children younger than them or toward their own peers.

LITTLE FRUMIE was five years old and in Pre-1A, She began complaining of headaches and stomachaches each morning when she got up. The pediatrician noticed a little weight loss but nothing significant. She told Frumie's mother to ignore it.

During the Pesach seder, when her father asked her what she wanted as an *afikoman* present, Frumie replied, "A briefcase with a lock." Startled, he asked why she needed a new briefcase. The one she had was still fine. And why the lock?

Big round tears rolled down Frumie's cheeks, and her lower lip quivered. It was difficult for her to answer as huge waves of terror shook her body like a volcano. Through the tears she stammered, "This way the big shots won't steal my snack and sandwich every day."

Both parents stared at their daughter in shock. Frumie was allergic to milk products and therefore could not eat the school lunch. Each day her mother prepared her a tasty lunch and a snack. To think that kids stole her food, leaving Frumie hungry all day, left her speechless. No wonder little Frumie hated school and awoke with aches each morning. Didn't the teacher see? Didn't the bigger kids know it is an *aveirah* to steal? Why hadn't Frumie told her parents about this before? Why didn't she at least complain to the teacher?

Children by and large don't report frightening experiences to parents for fear of being blamed for the problem. Or the bullies may have threatened and frightened the child into silence.

Parents and teachers need not keep surveillance on every single thing that goes on. It would be counterproductive and an unhealthy intrusion into the lives of the children who need to learn to fend for themselves. However, teachers should not shut down the minute class is over. One eye should at all times be focused on the students, regardless of their age and stage in life.

PINCHAS ATTENDS seventh grade in a typical yeshivah. But what happens to him each day is hopefully not typical. It was tacitly accepted among the boys that Big Moshe Meir, the class bully, could take whatever he wanted. If a classmate had a doughnut, he made sure to eat it in hiding before Big Moshe Meir saw it and grabbed it away from him. If Big Moshe Meir decided to put a kid in *cheirem*, when no one is permitted to speak to him, no one dared to contradict or defy him. Kids loved him and hated him at the same time. Some showered him with Parker pens, money, nosh, and yo-yos just to be favored by him for one day. This gift translated into being the captain of the baseball team during recess and being given the honor of choosing the boys and key positions for each team.

Pinchas wasn't stupid. He knew the rules and wouldn't dare refuse anything Big Moshe Meir asked of him. But trouble started when Big Moshe Meir asked him for two dollars and did not believe Pinchas did not have it. "Come on," he taunted him, "you always have money. Your father owns the corner grocery and always has cash."

"But I don't have any cash," protested Pinchas.

"Then go to your father and get some! And do it now!"

In all honesty, Pinchas would have done it in a minute, but no one was allowed to leave the school grounds without permission. If he got caught, he would have a lot of lying to do, since he could never tell on Big Moshe Meir. Besides, his father might not want to give him the money anyway, so why take the risk? The entire class watched in silence, wondering what would happen. Not a single boy came to his defense. They knew that siding with Pinchas instead of Big Moshe Meir meant not being able to play baseball for a whole week.

Just then the bell rang, signaling recess was over. But

Big Moshe Meir's booming voice paralyzed anyone from moving. "You are now in *cheirem* for two whole months. Anyone who speaks to you will be put into *cheirem*, too." Big Moshe Meir gave Pinchas a big shove and punched him in the face. A stream of blood oozed out of Pinchas's nose. He ran to the office to get some tissues to stop the bleeding. He did not tell the secretary how he really got the nosebleed, claiming he was prone to them. As the secretary reached for the tissues she said, "I always had nosebleeds when I was little, too."

Pinchas never related what happen to his parents or rebbe for fear of retaliation. His story would have never surfaced if Pinchas had not gotten depressed, his marks plunging from hundreds to fifties. His parents hired a tutor for him who was warm, intuitive, and interested in knowing why Pinchas always ate alone when he came to learn with him during lunchtime. With patience and a promise not to ever reveal the identity of Big Moshe Meir, Pinchas finally spilled the beans to his tutor, Aharon. Aharon kept his word.

The violence that has recently erupted in public schools should not be brushed off with "These things don't happen in *our* schools." Words shoot down students just like guns, killing their self-esteem, ego, and self-respect. Our children are also victimized by bullies, both in boys' yeshivos and in girls' schools.

Teachers, parents, principals, resource room teachers, and tutors should keep one eye open on the classwork and the other eye open for Big Moshe Meir. He exists in almost every school. Watch out for him and, by all means, don't be afraid to report on him and challenge him. If we adults don't protect our students and weed out the bullies, the violence that afflicts the public schools may not be as far away as you think.

The War on Ritalin

It seems that every era carries with it its own fads, myths, and controversial debates concerning child-rearing. Now that Dr. Spock is outdated and nursing has won the war as the healthiest form of providing baby's nutrition, we face the twenty-first-century issue of Ritalin as a way of controlling ADHD, a childhood behavioral disorder. Ritalin advocates support dispersing the medication like candy to every active child who disrupts the home or class. Ritalin opponents wouldn't give Ritalin to their child for fear of side effects, ignoring the fact that the side effects of a human bouncing ball has more physical and cognitive ill affects than Ritalin does.

How does a mother decide whom to believe?

As a mother, teacher, and children's therapist I have my own views on the Ritalin debate, and they don't conform to either the anti- or pro-Ritalin activists. My experience has been that Ritalin is a very individualized and personal decision. My decision depends on unbiased professional evaluation of the child's symptoms and prognosis. Depriving a child who really needs Ritalin is just as cruel as giving it to the child for no good reason. Before taking any side, I suggest parents do not jump to either conclusion due to their personal attitude toward medication. The rule of thumb is to abide by the needs of the child, not by the media, the latest fads, or your personal prejudice concerning medication in general.

When a child shows typical symptoms of ADHD, such as impulsivity, inability to carry out a task, irritability, bullying peers and siblings, impatience, and mood swings, do not immediately push for Ritalin. Long-term medication should not be a quick and conclusive solution for every difficult child. Parents must be aware that while a restless child may have ADHD, he may also not, despite all evidence of it. Fifty percent of children with the above symptoms are often suffering from some form of emotional disturbance, such as anxiety, depression, internal anger, post–traumatic stress disorder, lack of attention, or too much attention to the point of being spoiled. My philosophy is not to suggest Ritalin until these issues have first been dealt with and ruled out in therapy.

If consistent therapy has been ineffective in reducing the child's out-of-control behavior, it is probable that the child does have ADHD. At this point, I strongly advocate more intensive neurological testing, and almost always the prognosis is ADHD. Most likely, the doctor will prescribe Ritalin in addition to therapy. Not to give the child the medication at this point is negligent.

We have surprised dozens of parents who were sure their children had ADHD. Their children did not need to take Ritalin or any other type of medication. Play therapy or conventional therapy had improved the symptoms of the children's behavioral neuroses that mimicked ADHD. The anxious or attention-seeking child became satiated through therapy. His parents were taught how to boost his ego at home. Like the sun on a hot day, this melted away his negative behavior, his bullying, anxiety, anger, and impassivity.

Again, this is not to say that every child can be helped with therapy and healed of ADHD. Only when the child does not have the prognosis of ADHD will he respond so well to therapy treatment without the aid of medication. Children classified as ADHD need more than therapeutic intervention. They need Ritalin as well.

Let us remember that children cannot always help themselves. Often they need the helping hand of parents to lead them away from the dead end street of denial and onto the path of unbiased reality. Such a road, with the help of Hashem, will lead to trails of success. So grab the extended hand of your difficult child. Do what's best for him, not what is most convenient for you. Ultimately he will return your gesture with *nachas* to fill a lifetime.

Polishing a Diamond

IF YOU thought teaching a normal child took a lot of patience and talent, multiply those tools a hundred times over, and you will get an idea of what it's like to tutor or teach a mentally disturbed child. I did it twice.

The first time it was an after-school job. I would go to a group home and tutor an emotionally disturbed child. They gave me no instruction at all. The ideas and methods of teaching such a child had to come from me, and I was nervous.

Mendy was seven years old, hyperactive, and moody to the point where I never knew what to expect of him. One day he would greet me at the bus stop, smiling, jumping up and down in glee, hugging me. On other days, he would grab my briefcase as soon as I got off the bus and spill all its contents onto the floor, completely disregarding my shouts of "Stop that!"

I tutored him in *Chumash*. He would read a line and pretend not to know its English translation. "Tell me what it means," he would whine.

I was firm, telling him, "No, first you try to explain it to me, and then I will correct you if necessary."

On a good day, he would relent, and we would sometimes finish an entire passage. All along I would hold his
hand (he desperately needed affection), compliment him
on every correct word, and gently correct his wrong trans-
lations. I worked hard on my self-control to ignore his
constant fidgeting, wiping of his runny nose, dancing in
his seat, and steady drumming of his feet. This, after all,
was a "good day" — we were progressing academically.

On other days, he would run ahead of me after seeing
me get off the bus. When I would enter his room, Mendy
was nowhere to be seen. By the second week, I no longer
had to open every closet and door. I knew his favorite hiding
place was under his bed, and I didn't give him the satisfaction of bending down and begging him to come out. I already knew just how to let him know that I knew all his
games and would not give in to him. While he whined,
balked, and complained that I was mean for expecting him
to come out in two minutes flat or I would leave and go
home, I knew that deep down he needed the discipline. It
told him something few people ever did — that I cared about
him. No way in the world did he want me to go home
(which I had to do only one time to prove I was serious).

From the time school started that year in September
till I appeared six weeks later, he had already exhausted
three or four tutors. I wasn't a quitter, and Mendy thrived
on that knowledge like a baby who clings to his mother.
He loved me and didn't even know it. He didn't recognize
love because he had never loved anyone before, nor did
anyone ever love him. The concept of warmth and security, the outgrowth of love, never touched him.

Mendy had been an abused baby, abandoned at three,
shuttled from one foster home to another like a bouncing

ball. When he was placed in the residence home, he had a
rough time there, too. Three schools had expelled him for
misconduct, and the one that he was presently attending
was not happy with his behavior either. His IQ level
showed him to be quite bright, but emotionally and socially he was like a wild animal. If he did demonstrate
brightness, it was to figure out ways to drive people crazy.
No wonder no one felt warmth or love toward him. He returned every good gesture with unpredictable reactions
of anger, hate, and violence — just like he did with me
each day.

Something told me that consistency was like emotional oxygen to him. After two weeks of unsuccessful attempts to anger me, get me to quit, and tire me out, he realized I meant to stay. So we worked every day, slowly,
very slowly, with different games, tons of compliments,
hair tousling, prizes, and controlled temper on my part.
Progress started to set in. After a few weeks, I had him sitting on the chair almost every day struggling with a small
passage of *Chumash*.

One day I told him I loved him and would tutor him
till the end of the school year. First he laughed, saying I
was lying. Then he started crying and saying I was crazy. I
asked him why and he replied, "If you love a crazy, stupid
kid like me, you are crazy, too." I made it clear that I
thought I was an intelligent teacher and a normal person.
I told him I thought he was special in many ways and repeated that I loved him. He didn't believe me.

I decided to prove it. When his orphanage went on a
trip, I went along as a counselor, volunteering my whole
day. On the day of his birthday, I made him a small party
at the orphanage, begging other children to join us in the

creativity room. Most didn't like him and wouldn't come. The ones who did came for the cake and goodies. It made no difference to Mendy. He was happy. He smiled one of his rare smiles that tore my heart apart. I don't know if it was from pity or love, probably a combination of both. Some Sundays I took him to my house and introduced him to my sister and parents. My five sisters, all teenagers or married, accepted him without much commotion. He liked that. He felt normal.

The tutoring continued, and gradually I found him just a bit more predictable, just a bit less grinding on my nerves. By the middle of the winter, he no longer called me crazy when I told him I loved him. By the early spring, he no longer hid under the bed. He usually carried my briefcase into the room for me and looked inside with confidence for the treat that was always there. All along, we struggled with the lessons, braving each verse with patience and compliments.

Sometimes Mendy reminded me of the seals at the aquarium. Each time a seal did a trick, no matter how many times, it received a fish to eat as a prize. Mendy was the same way. Each word he learned called for some reinforcement.

Some days were so difficult I thought I couldn't last one more day. Knowing how much consistency meant to him, and especially my love, I never carried out my hidden thoughts. Today I'm glad, even proud of myself, for not quitting on him.

By June he was smiling a lot, fidgeting less in his seat, and able to tune in to the lessons almost on a daily basis. On some days, when he was especially good, I would play a game of checkers with him afterward, even if it meant staying late. He usually won, and that made him feel six feet tall.

The very last day I was there I bought him a goodbye gift, a watch. He loved it, although he grumbled that it was not waterproof. Like always, I didn't show any displeasure. I simply told him that I hoped he would think of me every time he looked at the watch. He finally smiled and shyly slid me a piece of paper as he said, "I have a present for you, too, but read it when you get home."

I got home exhausted as usual. Just before I closed the lights late at night, I remembered the note. I ran to my briefcase to get it. It read, "Dear Rachel, I love you. I love you more than I love myself. Love, Mendy."

For years, I kept that precious scrap of paper in my wallet until a few years ago, when my wallet was stolen with the note inside it.

Mendy taught me that patience, discipline, consistency, love, and more love are the keys that open the passageway to even the most unreachable child's heart. The lesson never lost its impact on me. It remains my guideline to healing other disturbed children. To this day, Mendy is still in my heart. Often I think of him, hoping and praying that my efforts remain with him as long as he remains in my heart, which is forever.

Today, twenty-two years later, I think of him as a raw diamond that needed a lot of polishing, so much so that my hand hurt from the rubbing. But the gleam, the beauty, the sparkle, hopefully still shine.

Discipline without Hurting

Most educators agree that too much discipline can be harmful to the emotional welfare of a child, while too little discipline can spoil the child and cause undue emotional harm. How to find the right balance is only one task of the parents. Once a parent recognizes the need for discipline, another question arises: how does one punish a two-year-old, a ten-year-old, a teenager? Should a mother use one standard form of reinforcement for all her children regardless of age and personality?

Research has shown that the more consistently punishment is applied (one that works for that particular child), the less the need to punish altogether. In short, two approaches need to be used simultaneously: flexibility — the willingness to accept the fact that different children may need different kinds and different levels of reinforcement — and consistency.

Timeout

Perhaps no single reinforcement has won more popularity than timeout. Timeout is removing a child from a conflicting environment. If a child refuses to listen to his mother and begins to shout or hit, the parents' best course of action is to say, "I understand that you are upset, but your behavior is unacceptable. If you do not stop this immediately (or in two minutes), you will have to go to your room." If the child does not stop acting up, the parent must carry out her threat and remove the child, either voluntarily or involuntarily. Often the mother's tone of voice in commanding the child to leave the room and go to the designated area is more important than the content of her words. Her tone should be firm, the eye contact direct, and she should show little or no trace of anger. Her face should convey a no-nonsense look.

The message may have to be repeated several times, especially at the beginning. Timeout can be a designated chair, the steps leading to the upstairs bedroom, or the youngster's bedroom. By no means should it be a dark closet. The length of time the child stays in the timeout area varies according to age. A two-year-old should be put into the designated area for no longer than five minutes, while a ten-year-old can remain ten to fifteen minutes. The idea is to improve behavior, not to frighten the child. An exasperated mother relates:

> You have no idea how much time, anger, and energy the timeout method of discipline has saved me. Before I used timeout, I used to scream and shout all day. But no one listened to me. They had become immune to my yelling. My next choice of action was hitting, and this became the disciplinary method of the day. First I found myself shouting, and when that didn't help, I lost my temper and hit the child, more out of frustration than as a punishment. It didn't even help. I would end up feeling miserable and tired, and the toys would still be all over the floor.
>
> At night, when the children were asleep, I would look at their innocent faces and cry in guilt and shame. Why did I

yell at them so much? They were really adorable children. Why did I hit them so much when I truly loved them? I felt so inadequate, so lost and helpless. I was sure it was all my fault. If I were a good mother, I would surely know how to in-still discipline into my children without berating, screaming, or hitting them. I decided to seek help the day I read a slogan that jolted me into questioning my attitudes toward disci-pline. It read: "Are you hitting your child to improve his be-havior or is it a disguise for doing your anger a favor?"

A social worker from the ODA Health Center taught me how to use timeout effectively. I needed a lot of support at first, since the concept was so foreign to me. Today my chil-dren no longer control the environment or my moods. I con-trol their environment. And guess what? As an unexpected surprise, the children's mood has changed, too. They are hap-pier and more cooperative. Now, when I look at my sleeping children, I am filled with security and happiness. I thank Hashem for helping me to be the kind of mother I had always wanted to be.

This mother was successful with timeout because she had the strength and perseverance to stick it out during the most dif-ficult period — the beginning. Perhaps no area of parenting tests a mother's strength of character as much as the early stage of in-stituting timeout into the family structure. During this begin-ning stage, the child will test the parent countless times to see how serious she is. The child's initial impulse will be to balk, scream, threaten, or pretend he loves timeout. However, even-tually the child will gain more respect for his mother and de-velop a deep sense of security, knowing that she is stronger than he. He will feel secure that his mother can take care of him in case of danger. She is strong and solid, someone to lean on in case of trouble. While he will not verbalize these sentiments, since he may not even be aware of them on a conscious level, his improved behavior and happier disposition will bear witness to his genuine feelings.

The father's support is a must during this critical time. The child will watch the father's reaction to determine his own reaction regarding cooperation.

With time, the child will resist less and less when told to go to the designated timeout areas. If, however, the mother fails to be consistent and fluctuates, sometimes giving in to the protests of the child, this disciplinary measure will not work. On the contrary, it will become a long power struggle between mother and child. And both mother and child will be the losers.

The Eight-Year-Old Arsonist

I COULDN'T blame Mrs. K. for wanting to send eight-year-old Pinchas back to where he had come from, a home for orphaned children in Israel. In the four months that Pinchas had stayed with her and her family, they had survived two fires, both started by Pinchas, bruised legs, and black-and-blue marks on their hands.

When little Pinchas first came to them, they were ready to give him the entire world and even more in exchange for the opportunity to love a child. They had prayed for ten years for a child of their own but it never happened. A great kabbalist in Jerusalem advised them, "Adopt a needy child from Israel. In this *zechus*, you will have children of your own."

The day I met Mrs. K. she was reconsidering her desire to bring any child into this world. Maybe having children was not as wonderful as people made it out to be. Maybe they had been better off before, when there was normalcy and order in the home. Since Pinchas had joined them, they had lost all semblance of routine. The house revolved around the boy's bouts of physical violence, chilling screams, and lack of basic living skills.

Pinchas didn't talk. He had never mastered language other than growling sounds. He also had not made the normal transition from diapers to underwear. Interestingly, this situation appeared not to bother him at all. In fact, he diapered himself! After soiling the diaper, he would matter-of-factly take a new diaper from the carton under his bed and promptly proceed to clean and change himself. If not for the odor the K.'s wouldn't have cared. They had far more serious issues to deal with — such as his pyromania. Pinchas hoarded matches in every pocket of his pants like a starving man hoards bread. Some were new, some were used, but they were all dangerous.

The first fire occurred on Friday night when Mrs. K. lay down to rest for a few minutes after candle lighting. Luckily her neighbor knocked on the door to visit her just at the exact moment when Pinchas was lighting a match, taking fire from the Shabbos candles. The knock jolted him, and he frantically threw the burning match onto the floor. Instinctively, he stamped his foot on the burning match but not before the wooden parquet was scorched black, telling a story he could neither verbalize nor hide.

The second fire occurred just two days before Mrs. K. came to see me. She was very careful not to leave Pinchas alone for even a minute. However, when her mother called one night during suppertime, she lowered her guard just long enough for Pinchas to poke a match under the pot of boiling soup. As soon as the match ignited, Mrs. K. screamed out, "Stop!" But it was too late. This time the flames leaped onto Pinchas's shirt, engulfing him like a human torch. Mrs. K. grabbed towels, threw

Pinchas to the ground, and quickly extinguished the dancing flames before they reached Pinchas's body.

Mrs. K. had tried almost everything to help Pinchas — vitamins, a sugar-free diet, weekly chiropractic sessions, holistic homeopathic therapies. Play therapy was Mrs. K.'s last attempt to help Pinchas before washing her hands of the whole business. If Pinchas could learn to trust me and play out his pain, rage, and humiliation, he could, with God's help, make room for healthy habits to develop. Still, Mrs. K. was not sure she had the perseverance or resilience to try again. The thought of bringing him to me twice a week was more than Mrs. K. could handle.

"I'm sorry, but I don't have the strength anymore. Deep down I don't think I even want to succeed. I'm ready to send Pinchas back to the orphanage. I feel he would be better off there. There they controlled his fire-setting pranks much better. Each time he touched a match or attempted to go near a fire he was put into isolation for two days. The child is too sick," she said with finality, "to live in a normal society." Tears of defeat formed in her blue eyes.

What could I say? I understood Mrs. K. all too well and identified with her fears. What good was it to keep Pinchas out of an institution if he was capable of harming or even killing people? Still, I felt there was hope for him, if only they would give play therapy a chance. I nodded as she told me her plans to contact the orphanage and find a person with whom she could send the child back.

"Until he leaves," I begged, "please bring him every Monday and Thursday." There was no answer, just the ruffling sound of a coat being put on, and Mrs. K. was gone.

On Thursday, I sat staring at the clock. Would she bring Pinchas? I wondered. While I didn't blame her if she didn't, I wished with all my heart that she would. I kept my courage up by thinking of cases in which play therapy had reached the most unreachable of children.

At 9:15 the door opened, and I got my first look at Pinchas. Startled, I collected myself and spoke to the human bundle standing before me in a normal, matter-of-fact tone. "Here in the playroom, you can do as you wish. There are cars, tools, crayons, dolls, and tons of other toys."

The bundle began to snarl, "Crazy lady."

I reflected his speech calmly and continued. "During the time that you are here you may do anything you wish as long as no one gets hurt."

"Crazy lady! Crazy lady!" he hurled at me, fiery eyes glaring with anger. Sensing my uneasiness, Pinchas gained courage and crawled closer to me. "Crazy lady, crazy lady," he repeated with bitter vengeance that showered a mist of saliva onto my face.

Like a shooting star falling from the sky, I quickly lost my equilibrium and courage. I fought hard not to show my fear and to maintain a professional stance. I wished someone would knock on the door or that a fire drill would sound so I could just run out. But I refused to allow Pinchas to win the war of intimidating every single adult he met. I knew Pinchas needed someone to exert control over him, providing him what every child needs — security in a big, scary world. Without knowing it, he was testing the boundaries, begging someone to be stronger than him so he could feel safe.

I stayed put, forcing myself to say words I did not mean or feel. "If saying 'crazy lady' is what you wish to do, then continue doing it. I am glad that you are doing what you want and need to do. Here you may do whatever you wish."

Pinchas realized that he couldn't unnerve me or get me upset. He glanced at me to see if I was watching. I was, but not overtly, only sneaking glances at him from the corner of my eye. Pinchas felt safe.

He crawled to the doll corner and studied the dolls, bottles, doll house, and furniture. Finally he picked up a baby bottle filled with water from the shelf. Still on the floor, he crawled into a fetal position and began to drink the bottle with loud sucking sounds. As if pierced by a knife, my heart ached for this eight-year-old child who was rocking back and forth, letting out pitiful whimpering sounds. Softly I commented that Pinchas was now sucking a bottle.

Thankfully Pinchas didn't retaliate with "crazy lady." Instead, I sensed a certain peace — someone stronger than him cared enough to take the role of adult. With relief, he permitted himself to be the infant and toddler he never was. His eyes darted toward me. *Can I trust this lady?*

Pinchas continued to rock and nurture himself for most of the session that week and the next. Each day he slumped with relief unto the floor, sucking up all three bottles of water that I had prepared for the session. One day, when the last bottle was finished, there was still time left. I wondered if he had synchronized this or whether it was coincidental. I explained that he had finished drinking and there were still ten minutes left. Relieved, he flung his body onto the huge teddy bear that was sitting quietly in the corner. His voice cracked as he buried himself in the animal's stomach, sobbing, "Mama, Mama, Mama!"

So Pinchas was finally trusting me. Relief spread over me, mingled with intense pain for this heartbroken child. I restrained the crack in my voice as I once again verbalized what was happening. "The bear is Mama, and you are crying, 'Mama.' "

Pinchas continued his newfound activity, no longer caring to notice my verbal interventions. At this point, he was used to them and almost seemed to welcome them, trusting that I wouldn't make fun of him. I was simply stating what he was doing. This offered him insight into his actions and gave the message that someone cared. Pinchas was allowing me to give him attention.

During the next few sessions, Pinchas spent less time drinking the bottles, almost rushing through the ritual, and more time with the teddy bear. "Mama, Mama, Mama," he parroted again and again. While the word was always the same, the tone took on different aspects. Sometimes it sounding pleading, at other times it expressed deep pain, and lately it had begun to take on an angry tone, as if to reprimand or hit back angrily at his mother.

I realized that Pinchas was spending less time nurturing himself and more time venting his anger at his mother. This was intensified when he suddenly thrust the big teddy bear across the room, screaming, with tears streaming down his cheeks, "Mama! Mama!" Over and over he retrieved the teddy bear, only to throw it again and again with more momentum across the room, expelling his rage toward his mother for all the bad she done and all the good she had not done.

I continued to reflect his actions, and by now Pinchas welcomed me as a support system. Now we were a team. He trusted me to join his threatening, mixed-up world. He no longer felt alone. Someone, a stranger, had joined his journey of pain. Regardless of how infantile or silly he was, she accepted him naturally, as if he was like everyone else.

By the fifth week, the teddy bear–throwing had come to an almost complete halt, and Pinchas had moved on to a new activity. He would exchange his Pampers with the huge teddy bear's blue shorts. Expertly he slipped the Pamper out from under his pants and fit the Pampers onto the bear, taping it snugly in place. After he was done, he would smile with accomplishment. I smiled back and reflected what Pinchas had done with traces of respect and unconditional regard. Slipping the teddy bear's deep blue shorts over his own pants, he looked a funny sight. It was hard to hide a smile. Oblivious, Pinchas continued to diaper and rediaper the teddy bear in an almost compulsive manner.

I was startled when a foreign sound suddenly came from Pinchas. I didn't understand what was happening. Pinchas had raised his face, leaned his head backward, and exploded with gurgling noises that resembled strangled laughter. Pinchas was not one to give up. He continued to practice laughing, experimenting with the strange and foreign sounds. He looked so pathetically funny, bending backward, clutching the diapered teddy bear in his hand, gargling as one does with mouthwash.

Without warning, I burst into my own laughter,

forgetting to retrain my impulses and stay only with the reflection of his actions. Once I began, I could not stop. I worried that my outburst would dispel his trust in me.

I need not have worried. Pinchas was not offended. Instead he slowly came over to me and placed his small hand over my throat, gently touching, examining, and measuring the movements my laughter made. Then he put the same hand on his own throat, trying to copy my movements and sounds. In less than two minutes, we both burst into spontaneous healthy laughter. Pinchas had learned to laugh, and he loved it. Over and over he would point to the teddy bear wearing his Pamper, and we'd both burst into another bout of laughter. This continued until the session was up.

I was tempted to prolong the session or perhaps offer him two prizes instead of the one he received after each session, but I didn't. I knew that consistency was a vital tool in play therapy, and rewards for accomplishments were unacceptable. Instead, I once again summarized and reflected the events of the session.

Pinchas left happy, completely forgetting to take off the bear's deep blue shorts that hung over his long black pants. I said nothing. He walked out of the room for a moment and then quickly ran back again laughing in sheer delight, not the least bit embarrassed or intimidated. He gave the teddy bear back the shorts and shoved the pamper into his long pants.

Just by looking at Mrs. K.'s face in the eighth week I knew that great changes were happening at home. Pinchas soon refused to wear Pampers and spontaneously trained himself. Even more impressive was his new personality. Pinchas no longer screamed "Crazy lady" at everyone who dared to come close to him. He now interacted more normally, even engaging in play with other children. His progress was so dramatic, it seemed almost like a miracle.

All along, Mrs. K. was coached on how to offer him love without choking him, to discipline without hitting, and to promote further growth by validating his new strengths and encouraging more milestones, all the while setting limits.

The system in the playroom had not changed. It continued to offer him security and stability. His play, however, was vastly different. He now ignored the bottles and the doll corner and concentrated more on age-level activities such as playing with the cars or creating a Hatzalah scenario with the police and ambulance cars. Other times he would point to items, asking me to give their names. Magic Marker, Popsicle sticks, glue, stapler, paint. Once an item was identified, Pinchas never forgot it. A small part of me suspected that he already knew the words but needed me to say them. Permission to use these words was granted once I had verbalized each item. So I continued his game over and over until every item, including the wire extending from my telephone, was identified. It was little wonder to me that he was now speaking clearly, almost normally. The hissing speech was long forgotten, replaced by sweet, joyous sounds.

Mrs. K. reported that Pinchas was still hoarding matches, but he no longer lit them. She coaxed him into handing them over to her each night before bedtime and he did. Some were burnt matches found on the pavements. Others were only match heads collected from ashtrays in unknown places, while others were new and ready to be lit at any moment. Pinchas handed them all to Mrs. K., and she rewarded him with a hug and a smile.

I wasn't surprised when Mrs. K. told me a short while later, just three months after therapy had begun, that they had decided to keep him after all. Not only was Mrs K. finding Pinchas lovable, but she was thrilled with his rapid progress. In return, Pinchas accepted her love and began to respond like most normal eight-year-olds. While I cautioned Mrs. K. about a relapse, I myself did not see any evidence of it. Therapy was progressing gradually and successfully. I was sure God had granted me the chance to witness another miracle. We were both sure that Pinchas had given up his most dangerous habit.

We were wrong.

One day Pinchas was in his room playing with Lego when he heard the phone ring. Typical of abused children who jerk from any abrupt noise or nuance, Pinchas shot up with fear but quickly relaxed as the reality of safety took over. He went back to his Lego. But not for long. Once he got distracted, it was difficult for him to reengage. Besides, he was hearing loud voices emanating from downstairs, and anxiety once again swept over him. He had to check to make sure his mommy was all right. But he never made it downstairs. He could clearly hear an agitated voice, and he stopped to listen at the top of the stairs.

"No, Pinchas is not leaving immediately! What do you mean, his mother wants him back? And with no notice? Absolutely not!" There was silence for a moment, and Pinchas wondered who his mommy was talking to. Then he heard Mommy sob, "No, of course he isn't adopted. You know we kept canceling the appointment to your office because we weren't ready to adopt him. We held off because we weren't sure whether we could handle him. When his mother was ready, we were not. Now we're ready, and the mother is not?"

Pinchas's head felt heavy. The world was spinning around faster than a roller coaster. He held on to the railing of the steps and wobbled back into his room. His heart was pounding with loud thuds, but a voice in his mind screamed even louder, demanding attention. *Light the fire! End all the pain of the past and the future. Do it now, fast! You'll be doing yourself and the entire world a favor.*

Pinchas staggered to his dresser, pulled out the last drawer, and immediately found the book of matches he had hidden for just such an occasion. Quickly, before he could think and perhaps change his mind, Pinchas lit the match. The match ignited but broke in half and fizzled out. He had lit millions of matches before at the first try. Now his hands were just not cooperating.

Pinchas bit his lip in frustration, and beads of sweat trickled into his eyes. But Pinchas was not to be deterred. He had a few more matches, and this time he would light them slowly and carefully. Suddenly he heard Mommy shout, "Pinchas! Pinchas! Do I smell burning matches?" Mrs. K. ran up the steps two at a time.

Pinchas had to do something to hide his deed, and he had to do it fast. Mommy was coming. Things would be all right after all. But ingrained habit was stronger than his newfound emotional health. He swiftly swept the match against the matchbook hoping that, like the one before, this too would crumble. Immediately a glow of sparkling light ignited, shocking him into reality. But it was too late. The smell of burnt flesh held him spellbound. He could not extinguish the match, nor could he throw it down.

Mrs. K. burst into the room and thrust the burning match out of his hand, onto the carpeted floor. She would have quickly stepped on it if she wasn't busy running with Pinchas to the bathroom to pour cold water over his wound. in her haste, she completely forgot about the lit match on the carpet. Her concentration was invested in examining Pinchas's burns. Luckily they didn't look too bad. Two small blisters stabilized as the soothing cold water cooled the skin. Just as Mrs. K. sighed with relief, she looked up to see hungry flames in Pinchas's room, licking at the wooden furniture. There wasn't even time to call the fire department. She grabbed Pinchas and ran out of the house, screaming for help.

When it was all over, the entire top floor was burned and the bottom floor severely damaged from smoke and water. The first thought that came to her mind when she surveyed the destruction was *Thank God Pinchas is going back. I've had enough.*

I got suspicious when Pinchas and his mother didn't show up the next day. She hadn't even called to cancel. It was so unlike her. Just when I gave up on their coming, the two burst into my office. Immediately I knew what had happened. No words needed to be exchanged. I simply took Pinchas's limp, scorched hand in mine and gently directed Mrs. K., who was still in a state of shock, to a chair in the waiting room. The door closed, and I suddenly forgot what I was supposed to do. The methodology of play therapy left me entirely, and I just stared ahead, wondering if there was still hope for the child. Pinchas sat down on the big chair, his feet dangling. Then he began to speak, so low at first I could barely hear him.

"Send me back. Send me back. That is where I belong, with people who set fires just like me. Mommy doesn't deserve a crazy boy.

"Let her send me back to my crazy family. That is where I belong. There I could set fires if people get me angry. In Israel, I can be crazy, and no one would care because they are all the same, just like me. My mother locked me in a box when I got her angry and scratched my back with burning hot sticks when I didn't listen. And I never listened. I hate her."

I marveled at his courageous attempt to articulate his thoughts. The words were simple and often unclear, but he struggled on.

"Once she sent me out to steal fruit at the market, but I couldn't because it was raining and people were not out shopping. The *shuk* was empty, and I was afraid I would be caught. My mother got so angry at me. She said I was a bad boy. She had to punish me to teach me a lesson so she tied me to a tree for the entire night. In the morning, she sent me back to the *shuk*, and this time I stole many fruits. She said that now I was a good boy and let me sleep inside."

Silence swept over the office. Pinchas was relieved. Finally he had explained the reason for his crazy behavior. He was now resigned and ready to return to where he thought he belonged.

A ticket had been bought that morning, and a man who was going to Israel agreed to escort Pinchas back home. He would take him to the orphanage, but if his biological mother fought hard enough, there was little doubt in anyone's mind that Pinchas would soon be reunited with his family. I demanded that Pinchas be brought for therapy every single day until he was supposed to leave, and Mrs. K. did not protest. Perhaps she felt that she was giving him one last goodbye effort.

The sessions no longer centered around playing. Pinchas had come a long way from Pampers, unclear speech, and lunatic behavior. Even if he was going home, perhaps he would carry some of his gains with him. We spoke a lot. Mostly I did the talking and Pinchas listened. I wondered out loud if he could channel his anger, fears, and panic into something more constructive than setting fires. I suggested hitting, knocking, and biting the punching bag in the playroom.

Intentionally I got him angry over little things. I'd scream loudly and fiercely for him to stop dangling his feet back and forth. They made me nervous, I insisted in a rage. Poor Pinchas. I could see the healthy pink glow fade from his face as a blanket of white disappointment paled his face with fear and anger. He looked up at me.

He raised his eyes to me in challenge. For a moment, I was frightened as he leaped from his chair, his fists ready to claw me and teeth set in grinding motion. He reminded me of a wild animal, and I braced myself for his attack. But it never came. Instead, Pinchas slammed into the punching bag screaming, "Crazy lady! Crazy lady!" He punched harder and harder, panting and venting his anger.

"Good boy," I shouted. "Hit the punching bag! Hit the punching bag!"

For fifteen minutes Pinchas did just that. When he finished, he looked worse than a wounded animal, but a huge smile appeared on his face. "I did it! I did it!" he cheered. "Tomorrow get me angry again."

And I did. This time his shoelaces were untied, and I strongly reprimanded him. At first he didn't take my fake anger seriously and just grinned. But when I slipped the shoes off his feet and threw them into the wastebasket, he genuinely lost his composure. Like a broken vase, his face crumbled into a million fragments of anger, despair, and terror. Again he was about to lunge at me, but like the day before, he ran to the punching bag instead. His screams were ear-splitting, but I didn't stop him as he continued to bellow and punch with all his might. When he was finished, he whispered to me in gasps, "Can you tell Mommy to buy me a punching bag for my room? I promise to run to the punching bag and not to the matches. Please?"

I asked Mrs. K. about it, but she was sure it would not work. She felt it was one thing for him to be able to do it at the therapy session and another to control himself at home. I didn't blame her for refusing to try. Besides, she was busy shopping for his return trip home. In spite of her anger she wanted to make sure he had enough clothes to wear. She bought him enough clothes to last a month.

Regardless of how hard I tried, Mrs. K. refused to test Pinchas's ability to channel his anger from harmful outburst to more constructive means. She did buy a punching bag, but was afraid of Pinchas. She was careful not to upset him in any way, often giving in to him rather than risking the consequences of his anger.

Luckily there were plenty of chances for Pinchas to get angry on his own, without any help from anyone. They were living at Mr. K.'s parents' home because of the damage done by the fire. One day a neighbor came by to borrow some eggs. Upon seeing Pinchas, she cringed and ran out of the apartment shrieking. She had heard about Pinchas and was afraid of him.

Little Pinchas immediately lost the color in his face, and the pale shade of cruelty took over. Shaking fiercely, like a small fragile tree in the midst of a huge storm, he made his way to the punching bag and immediately began to scream, "Crazy lady! Crazy lady!" Mrs. K. came to check what he was so hysterical about and was surprised to see Pinchas attacking the punching bag rather than her or her mother-in-law. He was screaming, "I'm going to burn you, crazy lady. I'm going to bite you, crazy lady."

When they came the next day for their session, I immediately noticed a positive change. They were once again holding hands, and there was a grin on both faces. Again I tested Pinchas's anger, this time finding it was harder and harder to get him angry. I wasn't sure if the difficulty came from his knowledge that I was trying deliberately to anger him or if his anger had receded to a more normal level. When they left, Mrs. K. winked at me, signaling that she would try to anger him purposely that day.

I was nervous the entire evening. Each time the phone rang, I was sure it was Mrs. K. calling to let me know that Pinchas had failed the test. I usually fall asleep quickly, but that night I couldn't sleep a wink. I was jittery and restless. I could barely wait for the sun to rise and the day to begin.

I raced to work an hour before Pinchas's nine o'clock appointment. I spent that hour davening *shacharis* and saying *tehillim*. I beseeched Hashem to give Pinchas the strength he needed to fight his urge to set fires to himself and others. I had even pledged eighteen dollars for *tzedakah* by the time they arrived.

The huge smile on their faces told me that my prayers had been answered. Mrs. K. told Pinchas to relate to me how he ran to the punching bag the minute he felt himself get angry. He did it five times as Mrs. K. kept testing him again and again, not believing the way Pinchas had learned to manage his anger. I was so proud of Pinchas. I gave him his prize at the beginning of the session instead of at the end. I thought my heart would break as he explained that he had been saving his prizes from the entire week to take back as gifts to his siblings.

I wondered if Mrs. K. had changed her mind but was afraid to know so I kept silent. The weekend was long and thankfully busy. I even managed to forget about Pinchas and focus on a bar mitzvah lunch I was attending. I had a wonderful Shabbos and was almost reluctant to return to my turbulent office job on Monday. When I did, I was well rewarded.

Mrs. K. arrived without Pinchas. She had sent him to school and decided to chat with me instead. Over the weekend, Pinchas had three episodes of real anger (not intentionally triggered by Mrs. K.), and each time he had directed his rage at the punching bag, not stopping to rant until he had gained control of himself. I sighed with relief as Mrs. K. handed me a box. It was filled with new clothes. Did I know of someone who needed them? Pinchas had more than he could possibly wear, and she did laundry twice a week, not once a month.

Usually I hand clients tissues, but this time Mrs. K. handed the Kleenex to me as I cried with open relief. Pinchas was lucky to have been able to grow into an emotionally healthy boy. Mrs. K. was lucky to have a normal child to raise, and I was lucky for having learned so much from this experience. Perhaps the biggest lesson was knowing that abused children can be helped and taught to lead normal lives. I felt a lot more hope for children who came from normal homes but had a hard time dealing with the normal issues of life.

Promoting Self-Esteem — a Difficult Task

Self-esteem does to a person what a spring shower does to a flower. It makes the person emotionally happy, healthy, and self-sufficient. Without self-esteem, the person is in a state of constant confusion, feels depressed, and incorrectly assumes he is less worthy than others. His innate personality, strengths, and talents never blossom to full maturity. He remains stuck, like a bud that did not receive sufficient water to blossom into a flower.

The best time to shower human beings with self-esteem is when they are still buds — little children. If human beings do not receive sufficient self-esteem from their caretakers when they are young, it is difficult and sometimes impossible to integrate it as an adult.

Self-Esteem Is Instilled, Not Inborn

Parents play a major role in instilling self-esteem in their children in the same way that they do in teaching respect and morality. Simply put, if children aren't taught self-worth, they will grow up without it.

A child has no concept of who he is, what kind of person he is, and if his existence is of any value. These answers are defined to him by his parents, either verbally or through their interaction with him.

If children are accepted, approved, and respected for what they are, they will most likely acquire positive attitudes about themselves. If the significant people in their lives belittle, blame, curse, degrade, or reject them, they are likely to develop unfavorable attitudes about themselves that will be very difficult to change once formed. We adults hold the keys to these children's self-conceptions and identities.

Self-esteem can be boosted in various ways depending on the age, stage, and personality of the child. It takes experience and insight to apply appropriate techniques of strengthening self-esteem. Nevertheless, the job must be done if one wishes to produce self-confident children who will grow into emotionally healthy adults.

Boosting the self-worth of a young child by telling him how wonderful and precious he is will not spoil him if discipline and limit-setting is enforced as well. When discipline and self-confidence are instilled simultaneously, the child does not become self-centered. It merely makes him feel secure and comfortable about himself among his peers. Spoiling a child means giving in to all his demands and placing no restrictions on him. It is worthwhile to note that children with high self-esteem tend to have parents who enforce and clearly define limits, while children who are spoiled have little or no self-esteem.

Instilling Confidence Is Easier Said than Done

Most parents sincerely love their children and consciously want to give them security and self-esteem, but often they fall short of succeeding. Isn't wanting to be a good parent enough?

Unfortunately research has proven that wanting to do something and successfully carrying it out are two separate departments. The motivation of wishing to be able to do something is not enough of a criterion for success. Just as a person needs to learn how to be a dentist before he can begin drilling a tooth, a mother needs to learn how to instill self-confidence if she is to apply it effectively to the child.

Instilling self-esteem is especially tricky because different temperaments, stages, and ages need different types of self-esteem boosting. A baby is content with cuddling and being kissed; a four-year-old needs a lot of hugs and direct compliments such as "You are so good!" and "You are the best in the whole world!" As a child matures, the nature of the compliments and demonstrations of love (which are the major boosters of self-esteem) need to be amended. A second-grader doesn't need as many hugs, kisses, and open compliments as a three-year-old. He may still need physical affection, such as a hug or an arm around the shoulder, but in addition, he needs to be complimented on his successful performance either scholastically or in helping the parent or being kind to a sibling. Not validating his accomplishments is detrimental to his self-esteem.

The Child Who Is Made to Feel Different

Children suffering from low self-esteem may come from the best of homes, with parents who have gone to great lengths to provide needed therapies such as speech or occupational therapy. While the therapy has helped, the child has a poor self-image. This may happen because the child is plucked out of class several times a week and begins to feel as if something is wrong with him, that he is different from everyone else.

In this situation, therapy and tutoring become a double-edged sword. They may resolve the immediate problem, but at the same time they may create the feeling of being different. Children with strong egos can handle this. Others may suffer deeply from feelings of shame, frustration, and a loss of self-esteem, the most vital component for self-actualization.

Many of these students who have been successfully integrated into a regular classroom begin to cry at the drop of the hat, act out, or become depressed. Worse still, many mainstreamed children become social recluses since most of their free time was spent catching up on technical skills instead of promoting lifelong social skills, which can be obtained only through excessive interaction with peers.

Silence Speaks Louder than Words

Silence can give a child negative messages that his mother may not even entertain. The child incorrectly interprets silence to mean that he isn't worth being noticed. His efforts are in vain, because his successes are of no value. As a result, he feels worthless, hopeless, and unsure of himself.

> MRS. N. is a mother with very low self-esteem that interferes with her role as a mother. The message of being a worthless, unimportant person was instilled through neglect in the form of silence.
>
> "I know my parents never cared about me," she says. "They thought I was a nobody. My presence was as valueless as the sand on the beach where I played all day.
>
> "I remember the many evenings when it would begin to get dark. Other mothers would shout to their children to come in for supper and bedtime, but not my mother. She let me stay out as long as I felt like it. Whenever I felt

lonely and hungry, I would wander into the bungalow, take whatever was in the fridge, and fall asleep wherever I felt like it. Sometimes it was on the floor, other times on the porch bench, and once even on the beach. All this time my parents were home, but they rarely spoke to me. They were good, kind people who felt that children can take care of themselves if they are big enough to walk, talk, and run."

Poor little girl. In the name of freedom and independence, she received a message louder than words: "No one cares about me." It's no wonder that the child grew into an adult who feels inferior and insecure about herself and her children. Each time she takes her children out on the street, she is in a state of anxiety. *Am I dressed right? Do I look shabby? Do I look overdressed? What will I do if two-year-old Shloimy cries on the street? People will think I am a bad mother who cannot make her child happy. I will buy him ice cream, soda, and potato chips to keep him quiet.*

Her list of strategies to keep her children in order is endless. Later, when she reaches her house in relief, she is certain that people have noticed the ices stains on her toddler's shirt and now is upset that she can't even keep her kids clean.

Mrs. N. is in a chronic state of insecurity and anxiety because she was not told when and how to do things. She has no idea if her plans are good or bad, if her decisions are appropriate or not. In short, she cannot make her own decisions because she herself does not know what they are. Her adult life is a constant state of not knowing. To this day she struggles with the issues of identity confusion, feeling worthless and inferior to her peers, just as she did as a little girl on the beach.

Negative Attention Hurts, Too

The flip side is the child who grew up with too much criticism. Though the adult did not experience the silence Mrs. N. did, the verbal messages she received were detrimental. Mrs. G. can still hear her mother's voice in her mind like a tape recording: "You are lazy. You will never amount to anything. Your house will always be in chaos, because you have a lazy personality. Go, get out of here. Go play. Come back in twenty minutes, on the dot. Why can't you get hundreds like your sister Faige? Are you stupid or something? How come you always eat the wrong foods? You live on nosh. When you grow up, you will look like a house."

Today, as an adult, Mrs. G. admits that her mother had not really meant what she had said. She was simply trying her best to teach her how to become a self-sufficient adult. Unfortunately, knowing this information does not help dispel the deeply rooted feelings of insecurity Mrs. G. feels today as an adult and mother.

Children do not have the ability to differentiate between what a mother says and what she means. To them, the words spoken by the parents are the truth. They internalize the messages their parents tell them regardless of how silly they may sound to an adult. Later, when they grow up, they cannot shed the negative self-image instilled in them as children.

Typically, Mrs. G. never feels successful no matter how orderly her household is. She takes no pride and joy in her efforts. People tell her that her house is spotless, but she knows better. It is a mess. Neighbors tell her that she works too hard, but Mrs. G. thinks they are joking. To her it is obvious that she is lazy. To prove her point, she tells them that she washes the floor only twice a day. Her friends laugh at her silly responses and claim she is an efficient housekeeper. Mrs. G. wonders why they are complimenting her. Do they want something from her, perhaps, a favor? Do they feel sorry for her because she is such a *neb*? And so the list of obsessive conflicts continue to torment her in adult life — just the way they did when she was a child.

Can an Insecure Parent Instill Security in Her Children?

The good news is that a mother can instill self-confidence in her children if she understands the significance of raising emotionally healthy children. Learning to praise your children even though you weren't praised as a child is difficult, but not impossible. It is natural to repeat the pattern of parenting one received. However, if one is determined not to harm her children in the same way she was harmed, she must acknowledge her painful past and search out the areas where she continues to suffer from low self-esteem. The next step is to attend lectures, listen to tapes, observe other mothers, take classes on parenting, and learn the language of praise she herself was never taught.

Parents Are Not Always at Fault

It is easy to blame one's parents for not receiving sufficient attention, but the truth is that it isn't always the fault of the parents. Often a serious crisis makes it impossible for a mother to focus her attention appropriately on the child's emotional well-being. A typical situation is the sudden death of a close family member such as the death of a parent, sudden trauma, a long-term crisis, or a new baby taking up most of the mother's energy.

To meet the emotional needs of the developing child when the mother is unable to do so often means turning to other adult family members to help out. Perhaps the grand-parents do not feel too stressed out and can be called upon in a crisis. If this is impossible, aunts, relatives, neighbors, or friends should be asked to help out. Perhaps someone could do homework with the six-year-old even though his mother is staying in the hospital. Maybe an aunt could go to the child's Chanukah play, and a neighbor can dress her up for Purim so she does not feel left out.

If a parent provides alternate means of providing for the child's needs, the child will suffer little or no long-term inferiority complex. If the parents do not realize the importance of substitute parenting, they are risking the emotional well-being of the children. Mothers need to understand that a trauma in the home creates a similar trauma for the children as well.

Misconduct May Be a Symptom of Low Self-Esteem

If the attention and praise of the developing child stopped abruptly due to a long-term crisis, the child will continue to develop physically, but his emotional growth will lag behind. His maturity can be compared to an unbalanced scale. He may know the entire *Chumash* by heart, but he will be sad. Instead of verbally telling his mother, "Mommy, please give me attention, please notice me, tell me that you still love me," he will most likely resort to aggressive behavior. He may begin to fight with anyone who looks at him the wrong way, cry for the slightest reason, become excessively jealous of his siblings, wake up with nightmares, or wet his bed.

If parents are too busy to pick up the symptoms of depression, anxiety, or emotional neglect, the child's symptoms may progress. He may begin to suffer from psychosomatic illnesses, such as headaches, stomachaches, loss of appetite, insomnia, and lack of energy. In a desperate attempt to call for help, the child may exacerbate his misconduct. He may begin to steal, purposely violate religious rituals, have tantrums, or even strike out physically at his parents.

Hitting and punishment will not improve the behavior of the deprived child. On the contrary, it will encourage him to continue with his detrimental behavior. Just as a starving person would rather eat a moldy piece of bread than die of starvation, a child would rather receive attention in the form of punishment, such as being hit or being screamed at, than wither away from deprivation of attention. Children will always choose inappropriate attention over no attention at all.

In a survey taken of repeated offenders of antisocial behaviors, such as breaking the law, stealing, and robbing, it was revealed that 91 percent of teenagers who were repeatedly arrested for misconduct expressed feelings of being rejected, unrecognized, misunderstood, and invalidated in the home environment. Seeking to fill the void of not being loved and cared for, they turned to delinquency as a form of receiving attention. Just as a body will decay from lack of nourishment, a child's happy disposition, moral attributions, and emotional gains will decay from lack of consistent emotional stroking.

Boosting the self-esteem of the developing child is not an option, but an absolute necessity — perhaps the most vital ingredient in parenting.

The Little Girl Who Stopped Talking

IT WAS a typical lazy Thursday afternoon at the bungalow colony. At five o'clock, girls were playing jump rope,
mothers were preparing supper, and boys raced on their
speed bikes, threatening to plow down the toddlers who
stood in the way. The screeching tires sprayed dust as far
as ten feet away followed by shouts of "Get out of my
way!" Whimpering sounds of protest meant all was well; no
one had gotten hurt.

Eight-year-old Aviva glanced nervously at her two-
year-old sister pushing her toy baby carriage while she
was jumping to "JJ *Chalav Yisrael.*" Her mother had instructed her to keep an eye on little Blimie so that she
could lie down for a few minutes in the air-conditioned
bedroom. The temperature had risen well into the nine-
ties in the past week, which happened to be the Nine
Days. Everyone was suffering from heat exhaustion. Of
course, swimming was out of the question, and several
mothers took extra precautions not to travel anywhere
that was not absolutely necessary. They whispered that

tragedies were more likely to occur at this time, during the nine days of mourning before Tishah B'Av. Aviva was straining her eyes so hard searching for a glimpse of Blimie's red polka-dotted dress and hot-pink carriage that she was out after the second round. Ignoring the shouts of "You're out!" she cocked her head upward and stood on the stoop steps with a worried look on her face. Where was Blimie? Why didn't she see her? She was just here a minute ago.

"Blimie! Blimie!" she screamed. Two Blimies turned around, but none were Blimie Schwartz. Alarmed, she ran to her friends, grabbed the rope, and cried, "I can't find Blimie!"

Immediately Aviva mobilized the eight- to ten-year-olds and took charge. "Chanie, you run to the day-camp house. Leah, you run to the playground. Shaindy, you run to the laundry room." They ran, all along screaming Blimie's name louder and louder, but no childish voice echoed back.

Someone ran to get Mrs. Schwartz, who shouted to her neighbor to announce a colony search, while Aviva ran in the direction of the pool. A cold wave of terror ran down her spine as she vaguely remembered Blimie muttering that her baby needed a bath today. Could she have been so clever as to try to use the pool, knowing that Mommy had said no baths until *erev Shabbos* on account of the Nine Days?

"The pool!" she yelled to the crowd of ladies who rushed out of their bungalows to join the search. "Check the pool!" Twenty ladies flew to the pool, wearing sneakers or slippers, with aprons and *tichels* flying behind them, perspiration dotting their panicky faces.

The first one to arrive was Aviva. She stopped with a

painful thump against her ribs. The gate was locked shut. The fence was supposed to be baby-proof. But there, in a corner, was a tear in the metal — a tear just large enough for a two-year-old to crawl through...

On November 2, pale-faced Aviva was dragged into my play therapy room at the Bais Yaakov, where I worked as a child therapist. The two teachers were puffing as they introduced the resistant young client to me. I had been briefed earlier by the same two worried teachers who explained the horror of the trauma poor Aviva had sustained three months before.

At first, no one noticed anything strange about Aviva. The family was too occupied with the details of mourning, sitting shivah, and grieving for their lost baby who was pronounced DOA by the time Hatzalah brought her into the emergency room after forty-five minutes of trying to resuscitate her.

When Aviva entered school, she was quiet and never spoke. At first they assumed she was shy, like many other third-graders are during the first few weeks of school. When Mrs. Winter bumped into Aviva's second-grade teacher, she seized the opportunity to ask about Aviva's severe case of shyness. Mrs. Parnes was shocked and had Mrs. Winter repeat the child's name three times before grasping the situation.

"But Aviva always had the busiest mouth in the class," she insisted. "She was fun-loving and popular."

Their worst fears were confirmed when they called her mother. At home, too, she had become more quiet and sullen with each passing day. Her mother could not recall the last time she had spoken to her nor to anyone else.

Now that she thought about it, her daughter must have stopped talking just about the time the tragedy had occurred.

Now Aviva stood, leaning against the locked door, surveying the situation. A look of resignation crossed her face as our eyes met, and we greeted one another without uttering a sound. Softly I explained that the toys and arts and crafts in the room were hers to play with as she wished for forty-five minutes. She could do anything she liked or do nothing at all.

With a surprising show of confidence, Aviva strode over to the bin of markers and began to draw. I was expecting pictures of water, drowning people, or sad children drawn in ugly colors of brown and black. But Aviva had an agenda of her own, and it was nothing at all like I had expected. Astonished, I pondered the bright red, yellow, green, and blue colors she used to draw and color a magnificent Shabbos table laden with *bentchers*, challos, and wine. Children sat around the table with huge smiles in pretty Shabbos dresses.

I was perplexed. Was Aviva resisting therapy by convincing me that everything was fine and beautiful in her life? If so, it was simply a control issue, her refusing to lower her guard in an attempt to keep me away from her secret. I couldn't blame her really. Why should she allow a stranger to intrude in her private pain? On the other hand, maybe she was in blissful denial. Drawing pictures of happy times may be representing her deep wish to return to the good old days before tragedy struck the family and turned her life upside down.

We met for another session, and then another. Each session was a repeat of the first. Gorgeous children, beautiful parents, happy homes, smiling babies, and parks laden with green trees and baby carriages covered Aviva's drawings. By now I was pretty certain Aviva was not trying to avoid or shut me out. She had simply shut down her present life, pretending it did not exist. She was living her life as if nothing had happened. She even drew a birthday party and made seven candles on the cake, scribbling, in pretty colors, "Happy Birthday, Aviva." It was clear that she was living as if things today were as charming and wonderful as they were a year ago. Aviva giggled and I joined her as she cut and pasted pretty birthday hats onto the guests at the party. Aviva put scissors in my hand, letting me know she needed help in cutting a piece of the colorful cake onto everyone's plate.

While I was now certain that Aviva was living a pretend life, I was not going to break down her defense of denial. Denial often works well in warding deep pain that, like a volcano, is too dangerous to erupt. One has to be emotionally strong and ready to deal with the pain of guilt, regret, and depression that like burning lava periously oozes down the fragile heart. So I waited, playing along with her game. I accepted her pretty pictures with broad smiles of approval and acknowledged her denial unconditionally. Not that the waiting was easy. It wasn't. During each session I held myself back from blurting out, "Whom are you trying to fool anyway? Everyone knows your sister died and you are miserable. Why don't you just tell me or draw for me how much you miss her? Why don't you at least cry just once for the little soul that left this world?"

In play therapy, however, the child is the leader, expressing her feeling of the moment at her pace, not at the pace of the world or the therapist. Here in this room, Aviva was not judged or coerced into doing or not doing what she didn't want to do. The time in this little room was hers to utilize in any way she wished, giving full comfort and relief, devoid of any pressure. Eventually she would find the strength to confront her issues. At that time I, as the therapist, would put my own emotions and needs on the shelf and would concentrate unconditionally on validation, summarization, reflection, and encouragement. Patience was a must.

One day, I vaguely noticed that Aviva's picture was just a bit less colorful than usual. The following week, Aviva made a house, not red but brown with black windows. During the session, in which she drew dark clouds dripping with spots of rain instead of a bright yellow sun, I knew her denial was about to break. Ever so gently, I remarked on the picture. "I see that today there is no sun, only big clouds that fill the entire sky."

She looked up at me, fear in her eyes, searching my face for understanding and permission to let go of her denial. I nodded solemnly to match her emotional affect and noted aloud the dark brown house and windows all colored black.

Just as I was about to point out the rain, a blotch of water fell onto the paper, and then another blotch. Aviva was crying. My heart danced with ambivalent emotions — happiness that her denial was breaking and sadness at knowing that the road to recovery is filled with throbbing thorns of emotional pain.

I held my breath, waiting for the inevitable. Sure enough, Aviva's stream of tears turned into a storm of sobs and screams that pierced the quiet halls louder than a siren. Doors opened, teachers stuck their heads out, and I signaled to them all to go back to class and ignore the screams, which got louder and stronger with each passing second. Aviva's face, like a broken mirror, was distorted into a million fragments.

Unable to bear the torture, she began to attack herself, pounding at her stomach and pulling out patches of blond hair. I quickly sprang into action, holding her hands down and firmly but empathetically making it clear that self-destructive acts were not acceptable in the playroom. Poor Aviva. She hurled her hands away from me with the strength of an adult and ran under the sink. There she wrapped her arms around the blunt silver pipes for comfort and cried and screamed till it was time to go. I explained to her that next time she may again do as she wishes as long as no one gets hurt. I gently washed her face, held up a tissue for her to blow her nose, and patted her hair back into place as best as I could without a brush at hand.

I was reluctant to find out how things were doing at home or in class. I called no one and waited to see what the next session would bring. To my surprise, Aviva did not even go near the markers. Instead she went straight to the doll house and began rearranging the furniture. Chairs were turned upside down with adults popped into them, disoriented, with one hand up, one hand down, and feet flying in midair. Tables were laden with pennies, which she seemed to have brought for just this occasion, and a long line of people were waiting outside the door trying to get in. When she draped a napkin around the only mirror in the doll house, I realized that Aviva was playing out the days of the shivah.

The next day I met Mrs. Winter in the lunchroom. I

tried to avoid her, but she ran after me. "Mrs. Schmidt, I must speak to you. Did you know that Aviva spoke to me yesterday? She actually asked for a pencil in a whisper, and during recess I noticed her holding hands with another girl. They were whispering secrets into each other's ears."

I gasped in shock and asked Mrs. Winter to keep a diary of her progress with short one-line entries. Excited, I ran into my office and immediately dialed her mother's house. Maybe she, too, had seen some progress. Her request to Mrs. Winter were the first words she had spoken since seeing Blimie's body floating in the water five months before. The phone rang endlessly on the other line, and to my disappointment an answering machine picked up.

I was anxious about the next session and drank a cup of black coffee in an effort to sooth my nerves. When Aviva arrived, she took action immediately as if she had rehearsed it many times before. She ran to the sink, stuffed it with tissues, and let the water run for fifteen minutes. When it was full, she reached for a doll and threw it into the water. In no time, the limp doll floated to the top. Aviva stood staring, mesmerized for a long time. Her face portrayed no emotion. It was serious but flat. *Should I break the spell?* I wondered. *Or should I allow her to stand there?* Quietly I took a spot next to her and copied her quiet stance of just staring at the floating body. I would have reflected her feelings if I had a clue as to what they were.

After what seemed like an eternity, Aviva darted out of the room into the hallway and pressed the fire alarm in the hall with all her might. Immediately doors opened, and people came running to check out the fire. I tried to pry her hands away but could not. With the strength of steel, she was calling for help — help for her baby sister, Blimie. The entire floor was in an uproar by the time three adults removed her hand from the fire bell, and I quickly shoved her back into the safety of the playroom before the roars of adult anger could reach her.

Within minutes I heard the announcement of "False alarm" over the mike, but Aviva didn't hear. She was busier than ever, blowing, or rather spitting, air into the mouth of the baby doll so fiercely that I was afraid it would fall out of her hand. It didn't. After all her strength was spent, she gently placed the dead doll into my hands for safekeeping while she looked around the room as if she had never seen it before. I wondered out loud what she was looking for and soon found out.

On the top shelf was an empty box that once held staples. She took it down, grabbed the baby doll, and stuck her into the small cardboard coffin. All along, I verbalized what she was doing, paving the way for her to continue her precious work. As soon as she was satisfied that the baby was Scotch-taped securely in the box, she took a marker and wrote in childish print, "Goodbye, Blimie." With that done and a look of satisfaction on her face, she hid the box deep in the recesses of two strong metal bookcases. Time was up and she was relieved to go.

It hadn't been an easy session, though she was acting brave and almost matter-of-fact about it. Like always, I said, "Goodbye. Have a nice day." Like always, she did not return my farewell. But what I did get was a look of gratitude and respect. With one last sigh of relief, she strode out of the room, her head just a bit higher than usual.

Soon Aviva was talking almost as well as she did last year — that is, to everyone but me. It bothered me that she did not let me enjoy any of her progress. Like the very first day, she still refused to say a single word to me. I met her one day walking into the lunchroom with her class. She was chattering with her partner when she spotted me. Immediately she withdrew from her friend and looked at me, frightened for a second at being caught talking but happy to see me. Seeing her confusion, I bailed her out with a natural "Hi, Aviva." She responded with a huge smile and a jolly wave of her hand. We both walked away satisfied. She was able to keep her pain and repression of the trauma safely with me, including her symptom of being electively mute, and I got my *nachas* of witnessing her speaking followed by a warm smile that spoke loudly and clearly the message of gratitude.

School was almost over, and we had two sessions left. The first she spent cleaning up the house, putting things into order, taking the draped napkin off the mirror, and using a hanger to push the coffin so deep into the crevices of the wall that even I could no longer see it. I wondered how she would end her last therapy session, since her work seemed to have been done.

Once again she surprised me. She picked up the markers once again and began to draw a new house. Like the first time, it was pretty and colorful. There was another birthday party going on, and again she gave me scissors to cut party hats and paper pieces of birthday cake. The only difference between this picture and the first was the number she had written on the cake. It was not a seven like the first time, but a bright eight. Words were unnecessary. I understood. Her life was once again happy and safe the way it had been last year at her seventh birthday party. As her session drew to an end, she did not throw the picture away as she had done with her previous drawings. Instead, she pointed to my briefcase, letting me know it was mine to keep. Happily I opened the zipper and allowed her to slip it in. I took one last glance as the timer rang, signaling that her time was up. Like a lady, she strode to the door and opened it without a word as I called my usual "Goodbye. Have a nice day." Instead of closing the door behind her, she suddenly turned around, ran to my arms, and gave me a big bear hug. Before I had a chance to hug her back, she was out the door.

The huge lump in my throat broke loose, and wet tears threatened to smear her pretty picture. I quickly zippered my briefcase and did what I could not do during my many sessions with Aviva. I gave attention to my own emotions and allowed myself a good cry. I wanted to run after her one last time to return her hug, but of course I didn't. In my heart of hearts I knew that Aviva no longer needed me. She was no longer a wounded bird who had lost her power to chirp. She was a brazen healthy bird who sang her songs to whomever she wished to sing them in the manner she wished. To some her songs were audible words. To others, like me, the trusted keeper of her trauma, it was a gesture of love that she sang — even louder than words.

12 to 18 Years

Identity versus Confusion

Adolescents face a civil war within themselves. Change becomes too rapid to integrate successfully without stress. They are unclear about their roles, identities, and physical growth. Parents who allow ample opportunities for teenagers to "try on different hats" while providing boundaries and setting limits promote healthy integration into the adult world.

Teenagers need both a balance of freedom and restrictions. Those who have poor role modeling, clearance to do whatever they wish, and too little guidance become confused about their roles in life. They are easy prey for delinquency and the wrong crowd. They grope for answers all through adulthood, never being content with their identity or role.

When I was sixteen, I thought my father was ignorant. When I turned twenty-one, I was amazed to find how much he had learned in five years.

— Mark Twain

Understanding the Needs
of Teenagers

The teenage years can be described as the best of times and the worse of times. It is the best of times because teenagers have the maturity to be independent, but the worst of times because what they do with their newfound maturity and independence often becomes a source of conflict to both themselves and their parents.

A mother who tries to understand her teenager and goes all out to be helpful with sincere advice may suddenly be met with "No thank you, I can do it myself." Another mother, who allows room for her teenager to make his own decisions, trusting the maturity of her child, will be accused, "You don't care about me. All you care about are the younger children." To make things even more complicated, a teenager can swing from one extreme to another. He may be excited about a planned event, such as visiting a favorite relative, and plunge into depression by nightfall, refusing to go anywhere. One wonders who suffers the growing pains more — the teenager or the parents.

Parents should not get frantic about their teenager's inconsistencies, moods, attitude, and behavior. It is important to understand just what teenagers are going through. Once they realize the emotional, mental, and physical growth teenagers experience, they will be more effective in providing support and protecting their sanity.

Teenagers Are Extremists

When one steps onto a scale, the needle of the scale sways back and forth before reaching the middle, the correct weight. So it is with teenagers. Before they can come to a middle ground, they often sway back and forth with regard to their personal needs and issues. This state of imbalance is extreme. And teenagers are extremists in almost everything.

One of the ways this manifests is in the time they spend grooming themselves, thinking that everyone is focused on what they are wearing and how they look. They notice a pimple on their chin and feel like a freak. They never have enough clothes because people already saw their entire wardrobe last year. Wearing the same clothes for two consecutive seasons is horribly embarrassing. Before they leave the house, their hair, clothing, and shoes must coordinate as if they were going out to meet Mashiach.

This intense interest in appearance stems from an imaginary audience that follows them around wherever they go. Trying to explain logically to the teenager that, although people in general notice appearance, it isn't the only thing they look at will do little to appease him or her.

To confuse matters even more, this same teenager who is so conscious about her appearance may very well live in a room that looks like a garbage dumping ground. Pointing out this contradiction will not yield much success. In all likelihood, it will either fall onto deaf ears or create a fertile battleground.

What is a mother to do? Her best course of action would be to ignore as much of her teenager's extreme behavior as possible. Only if she feels the behavior conflicts with her religious views should she put her foot down. But she shouldn't be surprised if her teenager refuses to understand, rebels, and gripes about the strict "prison-like" conditions in the house.

And if you think having survived one teenager makes you an expert in teenage parenting, wait for your next child to enter the stage. Suddenly you will realize your experience with the previous child barely resembles the extreme and conflicting behavior of your newest teenager.

Moodiness

Perhaps it is unfair to blame a teenager's moodiness on emotional instability. At no other stage in life is there such rapid physiological maturation as in the teenage years. It is during this time that the body transforms itself from that of a child to that of a mature adult. While this rapid change is normal, it can confuse your teenager and create feelings of ambivalence. On one hand, they desperately want to be considered grown up. On the other hand, adulthood may scare them. Also, part of this moodiness is due to hormones. The hormonal glands of teenagers are working overtime, contributing to the fluctuation in mood levels.

If your teenager "loves" spaghetti on Monday and eats an entire potful, don't be surprised to hear "What? Spaghetti again?" on Thursday. If your teenager is bubbling with enthusiasm about a new diet that will decrease her dress size from a twelve to an eight in four weeks, don't be astonished if you find her reaching for a third piece of chocolate cake on Shabbos. Instead of getting angry, impatient, or puzzled, it is better not to take them seriously (unless it conflicts with Torah values). Try to understand where these extremes are coming from, and you will realize it is a passing stage.

Friends

While friends are an important ingredient of socialization at all levels of growth, friends play the most important role to teenagers. It is through peers that teenagers find ample understanding and support in their struggle to become integrated into adult life. As an infant, the child depended mostly on his mother to fulfill his emotional and social needs. At school age, the child reaches out to classmates, who share the mother's emotional and social role. As teenagers, they rely more on peers to provide these same basic needs. It's not that they wish to throw their mother's emotional and social contact away forever; they merely need a period of time where their friends provide most of these social and emotional needs.

When teenagers become adults (most often when they become parents themselves), they once again reach out and appreciate their parents' experience. It is important for mothers to know that teenagers regard the opinion of peers even more important than their own, so don't take this behavior personally. It is a wise mother who is patient during these teenage years and does not force her views and opinions onto her teenager unless absolutely necessary.

Instead of a mother focusing on how much attention her teenager is giving her, she should use her energy to ensure that the group of friends her child looks to for validation and approval come from respectful families and are a positive influence on her child.

A Parent's Role in Instilling Self-Esteem

How are parents to instill self-esteem in their teenager if they are receiving mixed messages? They want to be there for their teenager, but their son or daughter doesn't really want a strong relationship with them. On the other hand, the teenager does need his parents to be there to lend support when he needs it.

The best course of action is to put on an imaginary raincoat so that you don't take your child's behavior too seriously. Let the ups and downs in his moods and his need for distance stream down your raincoat like raindrops without penetrating your emotions. Then there are times a parent *should* exert every ounce of strength to forcefully guide the teenager: if the teenager is doing things that are not within the constraints of the family's religious guidelines and if the child's depression doesn't lift and continues to deteriorate — if his mood takes a down swing and keeps going down.

In general, parents should be available to talk. These talks are best when they are informal, when baking cakes or challos together, taking brisk walks together, playing ping-pong, preparing for Shabbos together. Teenagers love to be consulted in family decisions, and parents should take advantage of their intelligence as well as the opportunity to interact. If parents make an effort, they can come up with quite a few issues that are appropriate to involve the teenager in and about which they can ask his opinion.

Perhaps more important than talking is listening. Many teenagers are chronic talkers and need an audience more than a debate partner. A parent listening to what they have to say, validating their opinions, and showing interest in what is important to them is vitally important to most teenagers. They use talk as a means of untangling personal feelings that are new to them. Being a sounding board at times is the most effective means of providing support. (In fact, this is important not only to teenagers, but to all children.)

To survive raising teenagers, mothers need to understand their child's makeup. Teenagers aren't purposely difficult; they are undergoing a difficult stage of life. It is advisable to view them as half adults, half children. When they behave like children, know that they still are children. When they behave like mature adults, relish the thought that they are growing up and *shep nachas*. When you get frustrated, remember that growing pains hurt for both parent and child. When you finally understand what teenagers are about and don't take everything they say or do too seriously and personally, you will be able to form an intimate adult relationship with your child when she outgrows that stage.

Are Good Grades
Destroying Our Students?

Teenagers go through many changes, both physical and emotional, until they become adults. While these caterpillars are transforming into butterflies, they are faced with agonizing pressures at school. They are struggling to keep up — with classmates, friends, grades, clothes, body changes, hormonal changes, and growth spurts. Belonging is as important to them as oxygen. At no other stage of life is the opinion of peers as important as in the teen years. The world revolves more around impressing peers than any other aspect of their lives.

Part of this is the need to get good grades in school. Grades become the most important factor in the whole world. Great marks and success become enmeshed. One cannot coexist without the other.

Our teenagers are not merely into marks; marks are into every aspect of their lives. If they don't do well, they feel ostracized. No wonder they stay up till two in the morning studying math with the same diligence the Chafetz Chaim employed in studying Gemara. This would be fine if math were their only subject. But the average high-school girl has sixteen different teachers for whom she needs to perform. Anything less than a ninety-seven percent on a test is as unacceptable as *chametz* on Pesach. No wonder the students plow on, sweat pouring down their brows, eyes half opened, as they fight the intense exhaustion that threatens to bring their grade down to a ninety if they dare fall asleep.

SURI, A fifteen-year-old who suffers from panic attacks, confides, "You have no idea how important marks are. There are two cliques in class — the smart one and the *neb* clique — and there is no in-between. Getting an eighty is a mortal sin. It immediately plunges you into the category of the *neb*s. I studied three nights for my algebra test and got a seventy-four. I refused to go to school for the next two days for fear of being asked what I got. My choice was to feign being ill or go to school and feel humiliated. I opted to act sick." A smirk crawls out of the corner of her mouth. It spreads to her entire face, and she bursts out laughing, trusting me with her secret. "I put the thermometer in hot water. I hope Hashem forgives me, but I was petrified to be classified as a *neb*.

"Last week I was so anxious when I realized I had left my notes in school that I hyperventilated. I lost my breath and turned red trying to catch some air. At first my family thought I was choking on something, but they soon realized that I was just having trouble breathing. My heart was racing so fast and hard, everyone in the room heard it. My mother called Hatzalah. I stayed three days in the hospital under observation. Every test under the sun came out negative. They declared I was suffering from panic attacks and sent me home with anti-anxiety medication.

FRUMIE IS sixteen years old and suffering from an eating disorder.

"I don't know what I'm doing here. I really don't. Therapy is for crazy people, not girls like me. I have tons of friends, get straight hundreds on all my tests."

She babbles on like a runaway train, not allowing a single word in, to prove her innocence. "I eat! I promise! Just because I lost fifteen pounds over the last year doesn't mean I'm sick. I was a size six and the fattest in the entire class. Now I'm a size four, and I feel so good about myself."

"But what about on Shabbos or at a *simchahs?* Don't you ever get tempted?"

She turns her face away to hide the sadness that spreads over her hollow cheeks. I know but do not reveal what her mother had told me. She had found suppositories in Frumie's bag, under her pillow, and in her coat pocket. Frumie turns away because she is embarrassed to tell me what she does if she commits the abomination of eating a piece of cake. She takes her suppositories, runs to the bathroom, and doesn't come out for a while.

The awkward silence that follows presses me to change the topic. I zoom in on the fact that she gets 105 percent on every test and congratulate her aloud on her amazing average. Expecting a smile or some other sign of acknowledgment, I am perplexed when she directs a sad gaze deep into my eyes. Our eyes remained locked in the chilling silence. I am confused about her thoughts and motives. I shudder as she jolts me with a sudden bitter cry. "Marks! Marks! Marks! That's all that matters at school. I study day and night for these marks. Marks are the only tickets to any fun or status in school. Believe me," she continues with conviction, "not getting good marks is worse than any crime in the world. Those nebby girls who don't have high averages don't get into plays, never sing a solo, don't get selected for conventions, never become candidates for G.O. They don't hold a single notable job! They are like the wallflowers."

My heart aches for her distress, her pain, her efforts, but I am sure she is exaggerating. Things couldn't be that bad. I try to hide my thoughts, but Frumie's sharp antennas pick up on them. Insulted, she quickly puts on her coat, but gives one last courageous try before exiting. With tears streaming down her face, she croaks in whispered desperation to be heard, "I know, because I was such a *neb* once upon a time in elementary school. The only job I got in the yearbook was photography, and no one liked or used my pictures anyway.

"During the summer before entering high school, I made a resolution never to go to sleep unless all my homework was done and I had studied for every single test. Once I sneaked out the back door after my parents went to sleep and spent an entire night studying for a final in the backyard. I have kept my vow, and I am now respected and popular. The fact that I can go without eating an entire day gives me even more prestige.

"Get real," she plows on, trying to make me understand, "I may not have a choice about getting super marks, but I can decide what goes into my mouth. So, like I said in the beginning, I have no problems or, rather, my problems are under control. Just tell my parents to leave me alone, because nothing in the world will make me give up my new status."

A decade ago, I treated a few anorexic teenagers. Today I

am flooded with teenagers who are clinically depressed, have panic attacks, bulimia, or anorexia. Almost every single one of them consider marks the number one pressure in their lives. They feel deep shame if their marks plunge into the eighties, claiming that only the smart girls are valued in school. One's worth is determined by her marks.

I'm not suggesting that schools create these emotional ills. I am merely wondering if school pressures may not be exacerbating the emotional vulnerabilities of normal teenagers and leading them to have mood swings, food disorders, image disorders, depression, and anxieties so severe as to warrant medication. Are we, the parents, responsible? When we ask that the schools provide the highest caliber of education possible, are we telling them that anything less than a ninety-eight average is unacceptable? Maybe our expectations are more magical than practical.

Perhaps it is time for the schools and parents to get together — not to accuse, not to point fingers, and certainly not to blame — but to reevaluate our priorities. We must acknowledge the fact that even if the competition is self-induced, it still can lead to panic attacks, anorexia, and other serious disorders. Perhaps your daughter is not affected by the pressure, but dozens of other students are. Let both schools and parents tell the girls, loudly, clearly, and sincerely, that an eighty is also a fine mark.

The truth is we have no choice. We must save our teenagers. Saying that Suri and Frumie's stories are isolated episodes is like allowing termites to destroy even the prettiest and strongest home, slowly but surely. Going into denial is not the solution.

This doesn't mean we should drop the importance of education. On the contrary, our involvement should emphasize love of learning and eradicate the taboo that getting good grades, like money, buys success. It's been proven that students who enjoy learning never stop being students, even long after the school years are over. Parents should be advised not to add to the pressure and to downplay the importance of marks at home. Teenagers need one place that is free of pressure.

Anorexia

Today a lot of emphasis is placed on being skinny. From skinny models to skinny stewardesses to skinny parents and skinny friends, it is no wonder teenagers are getting carried away with their own need to be skinny. Today skeletal means pretty. Years ago it meant you were poor. Not only that, but technology can make skinny actresses and models look even skinnier. Most often what we see in magazine pictures or ads is not real. The public does not see what goes on behind the camera, so they are fooled into believing that skinny is something they need to emulate in order to feel that they are beautiful. This message filters into the belief system of teenagers and often ticks off the buttons of anorexia in girls who are vulnerable.

The question most often asked is, *who* is vulnerable? Does heredity play a role or is it entirely peer pressure?

While almost anything can trigger the onset of anorexia, nothing does a better job than a specific type of pressure — the pressure of feeling stuck. All anorexics feel the extreme pressures of being trapped and helpless to control a complex environment. And they internalize their emotions rather than express them. When a teenager realizes that she cannot elicit her mother's attention or understanding, she may become anorexic as a cry of desperation. Anorexia, after all, is mostly about control or, rather, the inability to control a difficult situation. From a favorite grandparent dying of cancer to overcontrolling parents who leave little allowances for children to help in decision-making to peer pressure to diet to a repressed trauma that has never been resolved, all such circumstances have one root: the feeling of being stuck.

Instead of resorting to learned helplessness, anorexics cry out from their prison of entrapment by going on a hunger strike. While many friends are hearing the cry of desperation, they do not understand the cause of the desperate cry, and most often the anorexic doesn't either. Anorexia is very complicated, misleading, and difficult to cure because when asked what the problem is, the inevitable response is "Oh, nothing." When pressed for more information, anorexics will convince you that their life is milk and honey. With their savvy, smart demeanor they reject the help they so desperately need.

FAIGE IS beautiful, smart, and talented. When her mother, who is pregnant with the seventh child, aches from fatigue, all the children feign tiredness and go to sleep — except Faige, who stays awake and cleans up all by herself. When her friends ask how she maintains a hundred percent average with so little time to study, Faige replies, "My hobby is my family. When I'm not studying I'm helping my mother with the little ones. There is so much to do!" When her classmates begin to seriously diet, Faige goes overboard, counting calories, measuring fat content and food intake, and keeping long regimens of exercise. Before long, she is cutting her food into minute pieces and eating only a few morsels at a meal.

FIFTEEN-YEAR-OLD SHIFFY is pretty and confident. Her parents are wealthy, and she has every gadget one could possibly imagine. Her father's business keeps him away a lot, and her mother busies herself with volunteer work. From driving sick patients to and from hospitals to cooking for poor Russians, Shiffy's mother is at the forefront of every *chesed* program. In the eighth grade, Shiffy is chosen for valedictorian but refuses the privilege. Her father is away in South Africa on business, and her mother has already committed herself to a parlor meeting in their lovely home on the night of her graduation. To her friends' surprise, Shiffy insists that she hates to speak in front of an audience. People ask, "Don't you feel bad?" Stoically Shiffy replies, "No, not at all. I am much happier staying out of the limelight." Exactly one year later, she is diagnosed with bulimia, another form of eating disorder where one promotes self-induced vomiting to relieve oneself of the excess of food.

TZIPPORAH IS a great girl who gives lots of *nachas* to her family, which can trace itself back to the Vilna Gaon. Her parents own a shul to which dozens of members flock for daily minyanim. No one speaks at the Shabbos table unless it is related to a *devar Torah*. No one gets up unless it is to serve. The boys are forbidden to help, since they must fill every free moment with learning Torah. The girls cannot buy clothes; their mother sews them modest, appropriate dresses. They are discouraged from listening to lively music, not allowed to go out at night even with groups of friends, encouraged to daven *shacharis* and *minchah* each day, followed by Tehillim and reading from *The Midrash Says*.

Everyone in the family complains about the rigid rules, and all the kids finagle ways to have fun. Not Tzipporah. As the oldest, she must set an example, and she does. During Chol HaMo'ed Pesach, when the little ones go to the zoo and the older boys go to learn, Tzipporah stays home to bake Pesach cakes for the last days of *yom tov*. When her mother thanks her, she shrugs it off saying, "It's my pleasure to give flavor to the *yom tov*." One year and four months later, Tzipporah collapses in school, dehydrated, malnourished, and anemic. Diagnosis: anorexia.

Interestingly, all three girls are stuck in situations they feel they cannot get out of. The examples given are just a glimpse of their daily lives. Each episode in itself seems minute, but when you multiply them, you begin to see a pattern. Each is very good and never complains. Every one of them is a martyr who denies any discomfort in being self-sacrificing individuals. In reality, they are lying to themselves and everyone else and don't realize it. By insisting that everything is fine, they repress emotions of sadness, resentment, and anger in exchange for anorexia.

Why anorexia? Someone who is anorexic doesn't feel much of any emotion except mild depression which is also denied. Anorexics distract themselves from the pain of being controlled voluntarily or involuntarily by fasting all the time, exercising constantly, and obsessing about food they ate or did not eat almost every waking moment of the day. They feel tremendous guilt if they eat a normal meal, warranting severe consequences such as eating even less or using laxatives or vomiting to get rid of it. When worried relatives frown at their loss of weight, they smile and tell them not to worry about it.

But there is everything to worry about.

With time anorexia consumes everything they do, every morsel of food they put into their mouths. Every thought that comes to their mind revolves around the issue of eating. It is similar to being possessed with an uncontrollable cough over which they have no control. It controls them every minute of their waking hours.

Ironically, before anorexia they were extraordinarily good girls, controlled, poised, and eager to please. Once anorexia sets in, they become moody, uncooperative (with food intake), and great con artists in lying and denying their condition.

In severe cases, anorexia is not discovered until the teenager has passed the boundary of no return. It becomes a fatal illness of a fragmented heart tormented not with physical but emotional pain so severe that death seems the only escape. Way before the critical stage come physical signs of starvation: hair falling out, unwanted patches or nests of hair growing in odd parts of the body, obsession with calories, fat intake, and exercise, being chronically cold, fatigue, loss of menstrual cycle, clinical depression, distorted view of feeling fat, usage of laxatives, and vomiting. Loss of appetite becomes so severe that swallowing becomes a torturous experience.

The best cure for anorexia is to prevent it from occurring in the first place. Do not allow your child to be "too good." Insist that she go out with friends periodically instead of fulfilling everyone's emotional and physical needs. Promote open communication even if it isn't what you want to hear. You don't have to give in or agree all the time. It is not dangerous or permissive to reflect and validate your teenager's emotions while maintaining your position. Don't get too involved with business or work of any kind. Children are the greatest challenges and demand the most work from parents; they are not projects. If your child is ill or is experiencing an emotional dilemma, don't make her feel guilty for complaining. When a child is in a crisis or conflict about anything or anyone, listening and empathizing comes way before offering advice or *chizuk*.

While we don't want to make a sudden witch hunt and point fingers at every girl who wants to be slim, we shouldn't ignore obsessions surrounding food either. If you suspect your child has some form of eating disorder, don't blame yourself, don't cry, and don't degrade your child. Get her to talk about what is really bothering her, and listen real hard. If that doesn't work, don't be embarrassed to reach out for help. It may take a long time to reverse anorexia, but know that you will be giving your child a new life, free from obsessions about food and being perfect.

Forcing Maturity Is Like Overwatering Plants

THE FINKEL family was well off and enjoyed celebrating their *simchah*s in style. For their first bar mitzvah, they took two hundred guests to a five-star resort hotel. From brand-new black velvet yarmulkes that came in three sizes with the name of the bar mitzvah boy engraved on the inside to chocolate bars bearing Heshy's name to pictures taken of each couple, nothing was spared to make this event the bar mitzvah of the year. Not surprisingly, Heshy received over twenty thousand dollars in gifts, two thousand dollars worth of gift certificates, enough *sefarim* to set up his own library, stocks, bonds, a Casio, and a computer loaded with enough games and programs to keep him busy for months.

Five years and another spectacular bar mitzvah later, things have taken a drastic plunge in Mrs. Finkel's physical health. She was pregnant with a much-awaited fifth child. Her blood pressure was so high she suffered a ministroke, leaving her lethargic and depressed. Miraculously the fetus did not suffer any ill effects, but Mrs. Finkel was forced to stay in the hospital until delivery. In the fifth month of pregnancy, four weeks after the stroke, their third son, Efraim, had his bar mitzvah. Needless to say, it was quite different from his two older brothers'. Their mother was in the hospital and couldn't attend either the affair or the *kiddush*. The affair was held in the basement of a shul with only close family members. There was no fanfare. Helium balloons hung in the air and were drooping by the time the soup was served. The net worth of the gifts amounted to two thousand dollars and enough *sefarim* to fill one shelf.

Efraim tried to be a sport and understand that it was circumstances, not any fault in him, that made his affair seem like a bungalow compared to the mansions of his brothers. Still, when alone in his room, he cried all night. He didn't understand himself why he was crying. There was no reason to be upset. His mother had spoken to him earlier on the phone to wish him a hearty *mazel tov* on his entrance to manhood. But the more he tried to act like a man, the more he felt like a big baby. The more his mother tried to explain the logic behind his small bar mitzvah, the more he didn't understand it.

He could hear her voice now as he tossed and turned in bed: "Efraim, keep remembering that God has spared us a great tragedy. Perhaps it was only through the great merits of our grandparents who died *al kiddush Hashem* in the Holocaust that he performed such open miracles and saved the baby. Efraim, can you believe it? The baby seems to be perfectly fine. Every test came out normal. I am probably the first woman in history to have had a stroke while pregnant and still maintain a healthy baby. Efraim, we have made history."

Efraim tried to respond to his mother's enthusiasm but was met with rejection as he courageously tried to express his unhappiness. "But wouldn't it have been better if you didn't have the stroke in the first place? Wouldn't it have been better if you weren't pregnant at the time of my bar mitzvah?"

"Efraim, I am surprised at you," responded his mother. "Stop being so wrapped up in your own needs. Soon we will be blessed with a healthy baby. My physical health is in danger now, so I can't be with you. How can you not understand that? Do you want me to risk another stroke? It's a miracle that I came out of it only temporarily scarred. With physical therapy my mouth should be back to normal by the time the baby is born. Before you know it, we'll all be home, a big happy family."

"But what about my bar mitzvah?" blurted Efraim, desperate to be understood. "Don' t you feel even a little bad that you aren't here? Don't you see that I'm embarrassed in front of my friends who saw the elaborate bar mitzvahs of my brothers? Do you think it's fair that I won't have presents like theirs?"

His mother laughed off her son's concerns as trivial, and Efraim was left with the feeling that he was wrong to be upset. Now, lying in bed, questions continued to invade his mind. *My mother doesn't even feel sorry for me. She doesn't care about me at all. Am I supposed to take this in stride without any regrets or sympathy from her?* He had wanted to tell her that it was really she who was wrapped up in herself, not him, but kept quiet, knowing it was disrespectful and useless anyway. At the time, he felt proud that he had maintained some self-control. But now he cried, overwhelmed by his feelings of shame, regret, and self-pity. *As far as I'm concerned,* he figured, *I don't need this baby altogether. Why should it be more important than me? I came first, didn't I?*

Surprisingly, the next day his father took him for a ride, saying he wanted to explain things to make him feel better. After five minutes of conversation, Efraim wished he hadn't agreed to go.

"Efraim, I'm sorry, but we really have no choice, you know. I'm sorry your bar mitzvah is being pushed under the rug, but stop moping about it. Admit it. Isn't the health of the baby and Mommy more important than a big, lavish bar mitzvah? Yes, we all feel sorry, but our gratitude to Hashem far outweighs the sorrow we feel about the regular bar mitzvah arrangements. Besides, you're turning into a man just like your brothers did, just in a less lavish setting."

Efraim bit his lips painfully before agreeing that his father was right. Of course.

Two years later, Efraim began acting out in school. He punched kids as a first resort instead of trying to work it out, let his grades plunge, and gradually became a social recluse, refusing to return calls or even accept them when he was home. He spent his free hours at the bowling alley playing pinball.

One day, the police brought him back from his games drunk. They advised his parents to take the young man for help.

They did. His father's *rosh yeshivah* was in town for Shabbos, and Mr. Finkel made a special appointment to bring Efraim to speak with the *rav.* Much to Efraim's surprise, the *rosh yeshivah* did not rebuke him. Instead he said, "I'm wondering what is hurting you so much that you have to play pinball all day and drink to cover your pain."

Efraim was shocked. The *rosh yeshivah* was not bawling him out. He sounded friendly and nonthreatening as he continued, "I know that a *Yiddishe neshamah* doesn't turn away from the Torah without good reason. What is your reason for trying to substitute the security of the Torah with secular outlets?"

Efraim was dumbstruck, but much as he tried, he could not remember one bad thing happening in his life. He had only what to be grateful for, a miracle two-year-old sister who was healthy and smart for one thing.

The *rosh yeshivah*'s antennas went up. Why would a fifteen-year-old mention to him the miracle of his sister's health as the first thing to be grateful for? It sounded more like a statement parents make, not a fifteen-year-old sibling. He probed until Efraim spilled every detail of his bar mitzvah to the *rosh yeshivah*.

Was he surprised at the response that was begging for over two years to be heard! "I'm sorry, Efraim, that you couldn't have the same bar mitzvah as your brothers. It just isn't fair that you had to suffer the consequences of your mother's illness."

Huge tears appeared out of nowhere, and a heavy sigh erupted from his heart, unleashing two years of anguish and pain. The *rosh yeshivah* softly put his arm around Efraim and whispered, "Cry, my child, cry it all out. Your parents are adults. They can accept the disappointment of a small bar mitzvah, but you... You were merely a boy of thirteen. You could not be expected to view the situation with adult eyes, not yet anyway. Forcing a child into maturity can be very harmful. It leaves lifelong resentment toward *Yiddishkeit*. It isn't your fault that you've carried the resentments for so long. You aren't stubborn or rebellious. It's just that your angry feelings have never been resolved. No wonder you're trying to find satisfaction in a world of fantasy games. Your world of reality, your world of *frumkeit*, has given you a bad deal."

Perhaps it was to internalize and savor the security and strength that radiated from the *rosh yeshivah*'s kind words and supporting arm that kept Efraim's head down long after the tears and pain had ceased.

By the time *motza'ei Shabbos* had arrived, the *rosh yeshivah* had spoken to Efraim's parents and a meeting was taking place. First his father, then his mother, apologized and mourned his meager bar mitzvah celebration. His mother did not push her gratefulness of God's mercy on him. Instead, for the first time, she actually put herself in his place and admitted to feeling his pain of disappointment and embarrassment.

Efraim tried to protest that two years had already passed since then and it no longer mattered, but his mother refused to accept that. Her genuine pain was evident as she cried openly, embracing him with hugs of regret and empathy. Not once did she even hint at the word *but*. Not once did she say, "But I had no choice. But what was I supposed to do? But you must understand." Nor did his father give excuses to invalidate Efraim's pain. He apologized and did not venture into excuses like "If it would have been up to me, I would have had your bar mitzvah at the Kosel." Nor did he tell Efraim that he is now a grown man and expected to understand, not whine like a baby over a bar mitzvah when his mother and the baby were both in danger. He, too, stayed with Efraim's pain and validated his right to feeling left out and inferior.

No one can put his finger on what it was that transpired that night that made the difference, but from that evening on, Efraim became a new person. Gone was his angry look. Gone was his rebellious acting out. No longer did he go out and get drunk and spend six hours at a time playing pinball. Efraim became a content, serious young man, channeling his energy into learning and catching up on what he had lost over the past two years.

Taking a close look, it is evident that no great miracle occurred. His feelings were finally validated, void of "buts" and excuses. His parents finally lifted their adult expectations off his shoulders, allowing him to be a disappointed child. Now he was able to be guilt-free. The genuine empathy of his parents gave him the opportunity to let go of his anger, making room for new and happier emotions to set in.

The mistake the Finkels made and finally corrected is very common. Too often parents do not look through the eyes of the spiritually immature child but rather expect the children to see through adult eyes and embrace levels of *frumkeit* and maturity that took them decades to reach.

At times, when parents attempt to apologize for a circumstantial problem, they throw in so many excuses and "buts" that the empathy becomes completely diluted, almost lost. What remains are the excuses, not the genuine feelings of regret the child so desperately needs to deal with a loss, be it a missed vacation or small bar mitzvah or something more serious, such as illness, which makes it difficult for parents to meet the teenager's emotional needs.

When apologizing to a child or showing empathy, stay with the apology and discuss only the child's emotions. Don't place the burdens of the world on his shoulders too early by expecting him to understand. Nature has a way of dealing with forced maturity. It backfires, preventing the child from growing into a spiritually and emotionally healthy adult. Children, like plants, cannot be drowned with adult issues, high spiritual expectations, or adult understanding. Like the overwatered plant, they may mold and wither before ever blossoming, never knowing why they feel so rotten.

Yes, by all means, we cannot always make things fair or painless to children, but we don't have to add salt to their wounds either.

When Parents Are Enablers

It was happening again — yeshivah dropouts getting into trouble. This time it wasn't drugs or alcohol. It was theft in the most malicious and devious way. A seventeen-year-old and a twenty-year-old from good homes, prestigious families, stole a checkbook from a Boro Park doctor. Forging his signature, they went on a shopping spree. They looked like trustworthy customers, buying to their hearts' content. No one suspected they were using stolen checks. After all, they looked just like your son, nice *heimishe*-looking yeshivah boys, the types who probably delivered Tomchei Shabbos packages every Thursday night to needy families. Why would anyone suspect something unusual when they bought two pairs of new shoes at one store, new suits at another store, and video cameras and computers at another? But by the time they were finished, they had spent thousands of stolen dollars in a single day. They made their way home, drunk with the excitement of success, thinking they had beaten the system.

They were wrong.

Heshy Rubinstein, the founder of Kensington and Boro

Park Shomrim, was on their trail. Before the computers they had bought were put together or had a chance to be sold, the two boys were apprehended by his team of diligent agents, who work around the clock, seven days a week. Mr. Rubinstein got them to confess their crime, and he got more than he had bargained for. These two innocent-looking yeshivah boys were hard-core con artists who had stolen checks many times before. He called me to inform the public that if anyone is missing checks or has found checks being cashed in their names to call the Shomrim of Boro Park. He may be lucky enough to get either his merchandise or his money back.

What made me most angry about this episode was the way the families of these yeshivah boys were handling the problem. At first, they pretended not to notice the new clothes, equipment, and products that filtered into their homes. No questions were asked. Once the boys were arrested, they suddenly noticed the problem and sounded the alarm. Out of the woodwork came interested and caring family members, friends, aunts, cousins, and distant relatives, all begging the authorities not to publicize the names of the boys. "It would ruin my family's name," claimed one concerned relative. "It may impact on the *shidduchim* of my children," said another.

In the midst of all this turmoil, no one even mentioned rehabilitating the two boys through counseling or consulting mentors and *rabbanim*. The family's focus was on covering up the "unpleasant" episode so that everyone could go back to their routines. As for the parents, they continue to wear emotional sunglasses to shield them from seeing a future with their sons unloading truckloads of stolen merchandise.

Why weren't the parents taking notice? Why didn't they

stop them when it was in the infantile stage of unpaid for lollipops being brought into the house?

We need to understand how we can recognize the problems ourselves and reach out for help. Some parents are actually afraid of their children. From physical blows to verbal abuse, many mothers and fathers suffer in silence, bearing the shame in private rather than reporting their children. Other parents are ironically too involved helping worthy causes or doing community work to notice their own children crying out for attention. Some parents are so baffled they do not know how to handle their children's aggression or rebellion. They may yell, nag, punish, hit, put down, or demoralize their children, unaware that this will yield little positive results, only more serious transgressions.

The best response is removing one's defenses and understanding that teenage peer pressure is a lot stronger than the best parent-child relationship. Sometimes the best parents are faced with such issues. For this reason no parent should say, "It can't happen to me." We must pray daily for social safety for children and get involved in knowing the friends of our children. Be tough and demand to be told where your kids are at all times. But be respectful at the same time and never negate them with biting words such as, "You make my life miserable. You are a loser. You're a bad person."

Instead, appeal to their emotions with questions that can prompt positive results: "How do you think you would react in my position? How would you feel if this happened to your son? We want to help — tell us how. We cannot accept this kind of behavior. It must be stopped!" Use both hands, one to set limits and the other to build better communication. Tell your teenager, "Help us find ways to resolve this inappropriate behavior. Just like we don't accept non-kosher food in the house, we cannot accept your coming home at two o'clock in the morning. How do you suggest we deal with this problem?"

By attempting to elicit advice from your child, you are putting the responsibility of the negative episode onto his shoulders. You are also showing respect to your child with the message that you expect him to come home.

Continue with this approach until you receive some reasonable response. If you don't, reach out for professional help. Better that you should deal appropriately with your child than have your child take advantage of your weakness, naivete, and ignorance. Perhaps if parents understood that teenagers are torn between the need to be accepted by peers and their obligation to adhere to parental limitations, they will not lose their cool when episodes come up. Instead of yelling and putting their children down, they can take these opportunities of conflict to teach self-control and self-discipline. In return, they will find their teenager acting more respectful to them and others, while giving a taste of the dignity adulthood brings.

Children don't have to be perfect, but we cannot let them do whatever they want. We parents must take off our sunglasses, see the clouds, and find shelter for the entire family — before the storm erupts.

The Kallah Who Didn't Want to Get Married

I STARED at the pretty young *kallah* sitting across from me in my office. It was hard to take in what she was telling me.

"I don't want to get married. I know I got the best *shidduch* in the world and I'm supposed to be excited, but I'm not. What's so great about being married? It's work, work, work. And then more work! It's like going from the frying pan into the fire!" With that she began to cry. Her rhythmic, heaving sobs bore witness to her pain.

I searched for an instant solution to ease her tears and spotted her pretty jewelry. She wore a diamond-studded bracelet, an engagement ring boasting an oval diamond set in a nest of gold buds, and a necklace a quarter inch thick accented by a charm of glittering stones.

"I love your jewelry," I said. "It shows you are a *kallah* who is very much wanted, certainly by the *chasan's* family."

"Are you kidding?" she said incredulously. "I don't want jewelry. I don't want a husband. What I want is a vacation! I want to run away to the other end of the world and just be by myself for at least a year."

"A vacation? What for? What from?" I asked in surprise. This girl was really confusing me. She appeared to be the luckiest girl in the world, a girl who had everything going for her, and all she wanted was to run away. I was perplexed. I couldn't make heads or tails out of this sorrowful and confusing situation and seemed to be messing it up more by the minute.

Feeling angry at not being understood, she bounced out of her chair and muttered under her breath in sheer disgust, "This lady doesn't understand me, just like the rest of them." She left, slamming the door shut behind her. I was left feeling defeated. I tried to concentrate on other work, but she followed me home in my mind, and I couldn't get rid of her for days. Finally I decided to make an appointment with her mother and prayed she would consent to come.

She did.

Her demeanor impressed me. She appeared as a well-dressed woman who was genuinely interested in helping her daughter. She asked for suggestions and said she would do anything to make her daughter happy. I observed how she sat only halfway into the seat the way hurried and rushed people often do. I asked her for a family history.

There were eight children in the family, including a set of twins. The youngest was five months old and nursing. Esther, the *kallah*, was the oldest. With pride that bordered on embarrassment, the mother explained how Esther was her right hand, her left hand, and everything in between. Until recently they had lived in a two-bedroom apartment. Esther had slept with the three-year-old, who woke up every night to go to the bathroom. Two-year-old Nachum always awakened for a bottle. With a guilty edge, Esther's mother explained that it was Esther's idea that she sleep with the toddlers so that she, the mother, could devote herself to the infant.

"As a matter of fact," she added, "Esther is just too good. She didn't go to camp because she didn't want to leave me alone with all the children. Even when we went to the country and the summers were easier, Esther refused camp. She said she could not have a good time knowing how hard I was working. I know I should have insisted that she go anyway, but deep down I was happy that she helped me so much."

My mind began to churn with the reasons Esther didn't want to get married. I ask Mrs. L. if she expressed enough gratitude to her daughter all these years. Mrs. L. was sure that she did. She explained that a day didn't go by that Esther didn't hear her mother tell someone personally or on the phone that she would never have managed without Esther. "Yes," she affirmed, "Esther knows her worth. She hears it several times a day."

"But do you ever do something special just for Esther, like taking her to *simchahs*?" I asked. Mrs. L. explained that it was impossible for both of them to leave the babies at the same time, so naturally Esther volunteered to babysit so that she and her husband could both attend the *simchahs*.

I probed further. Did she ever make something just for Esther, like a Shabbos party for her friends? Again Mrs. L. shook her head and explained that Esther did not want to create extra work for her mother. Besides, if she entertained friends, she could not babysit, and her mother would not get her much needed rest.

It soon became clear why Esther did not want to get married. She had already raised a large family. She was too burned out to begin a second one. Besides, she confided in her next private session, "now my mother will have to work twice as hard without me. As for me, when my babies come, I won't even have an Esther to help me." Shame prompted her to place her hands over her face as she struggled to repress her guilty tears. "I've changed diapers so often, I feel like I've already done my share of diapering in this world. I wish I wouldn't feel guilty about that. I wish I looked forward to starting a new family. But I just want to run away to a peaceful place where I can eat a sandwich alone and not have to give a piece to Nachum or Heshy."

Luckily her wedding was still four months away. I prayed that with God's help we had enough time to give her back at least some of her childhood. Esther had insisted on helping, but unfortunately her mother was not aware of how important it was to validate, thank, and at times firmly refuse her unselfish help. Having her hear her mother tell friends that she could not manage alone only increased her feeling of responsibility to help. Her mother should have insisted that it was not Esther's duty to equally share in the responsibility of raising the children. Furthermore, her mother should have insisted that Esther socialize more despite her protests. I suggested to Esther's mother that she come for the sessions and that she bring along a notebook.

A new chapter opened in Esther's life. Her mother became a new mother and Esther in turn became a new *kallah*. Putting to practice the notes she had taken, Esther's mother began making up for the passed-over rewards and validation Esther desperately needed. She took Esther shopping for linen — alone — without shlepping the younger children along. She hired a babysitter so she could give Esther her undivided attention as they chose clothes, household goods, and a wedding gown together. To make this time completely stress free, Esther's mother stopped nursing her baby and left her in the care of a warm Russian babysitter who charged a fortune but did a great job.

Shopping was not all they did. Mrs. L. verbally expressed over lunch at the pizza store how she regretted having overused Esther. Now she would do things differently. She apologized for not being more assertive in forcing Esther to lead a more carefree life and allowing her to be a social teenager who went to camp and spent Shabbos with friends instead of babysitting. She bought her daughter gorgeous cutlery. Each piece was a symbol of gratitude. "This spoon," she told Esther, "is for staying up all those times to take Nachum to the bathroom. The forks are for the bottles you prepared in the middle of the night for Heshy. The knives are for all the babysitting you did so that I could go to *simchah*s." Esther began to laugh. Her mother continued, "When you have your own babies, I can just see Heshy and Nachum fighting to be allowed to babysit."

At first Esther was surprised and confused at the change in her mother. Suddenly she was taking charge, deciding where and when Esther was allowed to help in the house. Until now Esther had always decided, but no longer. Now her mother made these decisions and spent more time with her than with anyone else in the family. At first it felt strange and unfamiliar, almost scary. She wasn't used to being lavished with attention and having her needs met. She claimed there was no reason to change, but her mother insisted she knew better. Esther had a lot less household chores. Her mother insisted she go to friends every Shabbos afternoon. She didn't allow her to wake up even once for any child, not even when Heshy had chickenpox. Mother claimed that a *kallah* had to rest and be physically prepared for her wedding.

Interestingly enough, the less she did in the house, the more time Esther had to daydream about a spotless kitchen with new pots and pans. She spent evenings trying on her new clothes again and looking at herself in the mirror. She went on a diet and lost the seven pounds she had wanted desperately to lose for years. But most interesting, she no longer felt the intense need to run away. She felt as if she was away on a vacation. Gradually, very gradually, she began to look forward to her wedding. Gone was the strained expression on her face and the look of apprehension. A soft rose color glowed from her face as happiness radiated from her heart.

I saw her one last time a week before her wedding. Toward the end of the session, her head held high, she asked, "Why are things different at home? What did you tell my mother? She is a changed person and so am I. I can hardly wait for my wedding."

I smiled from the heart and wished her the best of luck as I stood up to signal that the session was over. She, too, stood up, made eye contact with me, and said, with smiling eyes, "I see that you aren't going to answer my questions. It's all right. You don't have to tell me your secrets.

But promise me that you'll spread this secret to every mother in the world, especially those who have oldest girls."

I agreed easily and reached for my computer as she fluttered out of my office resembling a beautiful, free butterfly. Sharing her story was the best possible way to keep my promise, so I began to write.

Young Adulthood

Intimacy versus Isolation

At this stage, adults are capable of forming long-term positive relationships with others. They can give to others without sacrificing themselves and at the same time receive without "taking over."

Other adults form relationships that are not healthy. One partner may be a giver or a taker, disrupting the equilibrium of an equal friendship, where the balances of give and take are defined and shared. Other adults may not be able to form any permanent relationships, while others will cling to an unhealthy relationship, paralyzed from making a change.

Marriage is for growth. By its very nature, marriage will continuously give you opportunities to develop your character.

— Rabbi Zelig Pliskin

What You Need to Know before Marriage

If you are getting married with the notion that in your house everything will be terrific and that you will be happy all the time, you are setting yourself up for a major disappointment. The fact is that no home is ever perfect and you cannot always be happy. Happiness is like the head of a turtle, peeking in and out many times before it decides to stay. Instant happiness is a myth taken from the fairy tales that suggest they "lived happily after" without saying how that is possible.

In real life, no two marriages are alike, so it's important not to look at the marriage of a friend, sibling, or parents and attempt to duplicate it. What makes your friend's spouse thrilled may create an allergic reaction in your own spouse. This happened with newlyweds Chaim and Faige.

CHAIM ALWAYS saw his father bring flowers to his mother for Shabbos and naturally did the same. Faige is too embarrassed to say she has severe allergies toward all living plants and sneezes fifty-two Shabbosos away before getting up the courage to tell her husband to stop buying her flowers.

Chaim comes from an immaculate home where everyone removes his shoes and dons slippers before entering the house. Faige's mother cleans the house once a week for Shabbos. Chaim tries hinting about the dishes that have been sitting in the sink for three days, but Faige does not pick up the cues. She has no notion as to why Chaim paces the floor with agitation. What he is thinking is, *I married a slob. The house smells, and she doesn't even notice. A good balabusta is more valuable than having a college degree. I can't take this anymore.*

Faige has her share of woes. She resents having to speak to her mother-in-law every day for the sake of her husband, who considers it basic etiquette. She buys her husband three new shirts for his birthday, and his face blanches when he sees the price tag of $7.99. She has no clue as to what she has done wrong, and Chaim insists he loves the shirts. Only later, when she thinks of looking at some of his unopened shirts bought before their marriage, does she understand. The price tags range from $29.99 to $49.99. *What a waste of money*, she thinks. *People are starving of hunger all over the world, and just one of Chaim's shirts can support ten families in China for a month.*

Chaim, in the name of being a good sport, and Faige, in the name of trying to be an accepting wife, do not speak to each other about their differences regarding spending money, housekeeping, or extended family obligations. They don't even know that they aren't communicating. All they are aware of is resentment, disappointment, and unfulfilled dreams.

Couples should talk about the similarities and differences

of their lifestyles before marriage. Couples who do not see each other much before marriage need to know that marriage does not make any spouse a mind reader. They cannot get married with expectations because most of them will just backfire, creating a traumatic beginning.

Don't expect your new wife or husband to know all your likes, dislikes, moods, and opinions. Nor should you think you know each other just because you are married. You both married for potential goodness and compatibility between the two of you, and the potential can take months and even years to bear fruit. Don't be disappointed if you don't see eye to eye on many issues, from politics to spending money. In most instances, both of you are right — there is no one way of doing just about anything. The rule of the thumb is, if it's not a halachic issue, both of you are right. You just have to decide between you which factors make one opinion of overriding concern. This means that one or both of you may have to give in a little to come to a decision. Bearing this in mind dispels the fear of divorce and never making it work.

Interestingly, Chaim and Faige dated for four months before they got engaged and went out regularly during the engagement. Why, then, were the issues of eating manners, spending money, and family obligations not discussed? Simply because during that time Faige always used a fork and knife properly when they went out. Her fiancé often spent money on their dates, since they'd eat at expensive restaurants, but Faige attributed this to the fact that there is a time for everything and the engagement period is when one indulges on trivialities. As for housekeeping, her house was cleaned every time he picked her up for a date.

No wonder they were both shocked when they got married and reality began to set in. The truth is that neither

Chaim nor Faige are to blame. No one told them that dating and being married is as different as day and night. They expected their marriage to be a continuation of their engagement, which was filled with shopping, fun, and talk on topics that alluded to "living happily ever after" when the *chuppah* was over.

TZIPPY AND Yaakov were the perfect engaged couple. They shared a love of music, art, writing, sports, and lifelong family commitment. Their eyes sparkled with the mutual love they had for each other. They felt that they had found their *bashert*. And they did. What they did not find was that the sparkle in their eyes lasted for no more than a few weeks.

They had their first major blowup when Tzippy felt her husband was leaving her to fend for herself each evening while he continued to do his business from home. Their dinner was interrupted every night by emergency calls that came in on the cell phone sitting between them as they ate.

One night, after the fourth emergency call, Tzippy lost her patience and cried straight into her soup, unnoticed by her husband, who was brainstorming as he gulped his soup in bliss. It was twenty-five minutes later, when wet-faced Tzippy had fallen asleep on the couch, never having served the roast, and Chaim had finally hung up, eager for the next course, when he discovered his wife asleep. Guilt filled him from head to toe. He remembered being told again and again by Tzippy how much she looked forward to spending time alone with him, and now she had cried herself to sleep and he hadn't even noticed. For a moment he wished she would enjoy talking on the phone as much as he did. So much pain and compromising would be spared. But in his heart of hearts, he knew this was unrealistic.

Both Tzippy and Yaakov need to understand that the longest engagement could not prepare them or expose them to what marriage is all about. It seemed to them that their bubble of love had burst like a balloon stuck with a pin. They didn't realize that they had never been "in love." What they felt was an infatuation for each other. The imagined love meant different things for each of them. For Yaakov it meant sharing his business and many friends with Tzippy on a daily basis. Tzippy imagined love to mean excluding the outside world, work included, and focusing solely on each other's needs, with daily long discussions and quiet, intimate dinners. Friends were important before marriage; there was no need for them when you had each other. Once married, there no longer existed a need for anyone other than each other.

Yaakov and Tzippy's situation is typical. They are good people, but they entered marriage with the wrong expectations. They went for marital counseling and learned to patch their balloon of love and inflate it once again, but this time with real expectations instead of infatuation. True love grows slowly like a seedling planted into the earth. Experiencing both hardships and positive events together, such as helping each other reach individual goals, the birth of a child, illness of a close family member, winning the lottery, and struggling to make ends meet, all contribute to bringing a couple closer. During these times, both good and bad, mature communication is a must. Talking forms the bond. With time, trusting love begins to burst through the earth, like a fragile rosebud, quivering with ambivalent emotions that speaks of fear of failure and the promise of full bloom, playing hide and seek many times before finally maturing into a full rose. And even then, the love needs to be constantly stoked like wood in a glowing fireplace.

Sensitivity, compromise, and giving make all the difference. For Yaakov this meant closing down all outside communication at certain times of the day. For Tzippy it meant finding someone other than her husband to fulfill her emotional needs. I knew the couple was making progress when Tzippy confided to me, "I felt like a leash around my husband's neck and hated myself for it. I decided to loosen the choking grip by inviting my friends for dinner, going shopping with my sister instead of my busy husband, and taking a hair-styling course to learn how to set wigs." I was further impressed when Yaakov made a commitment to take his wife out for a date once a week, free of all calls, to rekindle the sparkle in her eyes.

Interesting to note is that both couples married for good reasons, but both suffered similar difficulties. All four of the newlyweds married more to give than to get. But they did not give what their spouse wanted. More often they gave what they wanted to give, not what their spouse wanted to receive. This is not true giving. It is a form of narcissism covered with chocolate to look good. Often the spouse means well but is not aware of how negatively his selfishness is impacting on the partner.

Perhaps the biggest surprise for many couples is discovering how different they are in sleeping patterns, moods, ability to express themselves, and temperament. Again, infatuation or ignorance blinds the need to discuss these differences with a good friend or professionals. While most men are usually more introverted, women are usually more extroverted. Men in general have a harder time with emotional expression than women. Society frowns upon men who cry but accepts women who cry as part of life. Women have hormones that jump almost always at the wrong time, such as when they have to go to in-laws for a visit. Women in general need a lot more time at first to express intimacies. Men always win the race and can barely wait for the women to catch up with them. (Sometimes it happens sooner than expected, but that is not the norm.)

Usually both partners are good and normal (this excludes physical, verbal, or social abuse) but are very different when it comes to eating habits, cleanliness, opinion on politics, family systems, higher education, attitudes about *kollel*, mothers working, and spending money. When it comes to financial issues, it is not the amount of money available that determines how much one spends but rather how one prioritizes purchases. In the same vein, one *kollel* husband is valued and respected for learning Torah all day. In another home, he may be seen as a work dodger who takes advantage of his wife, expecting her to work and raise children.

It is important to know which family you are getting into before marriage, not after. For this reason premarital counseling, long talks with parents, and serious discussions with close friends who can be objectively honest are essential for every *chasan* and *kallah*. To hasten the cause-and-effect process of commitment, bonding, and a good marriage, two mature people must be prepared to give more than to get. A *bayis ne'eman* is never a given gift; it is the successful perseverance of two working people blessed with Hashem's Presence dwelling in their midst.

Surviving Motherhood

Perhaps no career in the world is as encompassing as the role of mother. At 7:45 A.M., Faige begins her job as the conductor in charge at Grand Central Station. Little Yossele leaves on the 7:45 A.M. bus, Breindy's bus leaves at 8:00 A.M., and Moishele, who is up next and should be big enough to wait at the bus stop by himself, insists with pitiful tears that he dreamed a kidnapper was about to pull him into a car.

So Faige runs, huffing and puffing like an express train, to meet the 7:45 A.M. bus at Lee Avenue. The 8:00 A.M. bus stops on the corner of Rutledge Street. Moishele clings to Faige's hand until his bus arrives, anywhere between 8:10 and 9:00. His stop is a block away, because the bus driver refuses to enter the busy intersection at Lee Avenue and insists the boys walk to Harrison Avenue. This is no big deal for the average nine-year-old, but for Moishele it is like walking through the desert alone. The driver, a Russian immigrant, apologizes daily for being late. He doesn't know the streets of Williamsburg yet and confuses Rutledge Street with Heyward Street.

At 9:15, Faige begins her trek back to her house, but her pace is held up by baby Chanie, who has fallen into a peaceful morning nap. She is only eight months old, but weighs a ton.

Faige shifts her from the left side to the right, silently praying, *Hashem, please don't let her wake up.* Of course Chanie wakes up half a block away from home. She strengthens her lungs with loud screams, competing with the horns of the cars and buses that struggle to pass each other in the morning rush hour.

A bus driver feels sorry for the mother and offers her a ride down the block. The ride is not free. The driver feels obligated to offer important advice: "I raised two children in Russia. There a mother would never take a crying baby out on the street so early in the morning. Probably the baby is hungry..."

"I'll get off now, thank you."

"In Russia the babies were cared for..."

The four-room apartment never looked so inviting. The beds are unmade, banana peels are on the floor, but Faige is home at last. Her conducting job is over for the day. No, she reminds herself. At three o'clock, she will return to the bus stops to work her afternoon shift.

In the meantime, the laundry is overflowing from the hamper, begging for attention, while the chicken for supper is still in the freezer. Faige had forgotten to take it out to defrost last night. The baby has an appointment for her polio shot today. Faige knows a scheduled appointment means it can take anywhere between one and three hours from beginning to end just for a shot. For a second she entertains the thought, *Too bad Moishele didn't wheeze last night. Then I could have killed two birds with one stone.*

Just as she is beginning to feel guilty for having such nasty thoughts, Faige remembers that she forgot to give him his medication this morning. Moishele will wheeze tonight, and then have to be taken tomorrow to be monitored.

As she reaches for her first cup of coffee, she debates whether to call her mother and cancel their scheduled outing to Boro Park tomorrow to buy fabric. She knows already what her mother will say: "I didn't see the reason to go to Boro Park for fabric anyway. It seems so odd. Today's mothers give themselves extra work. The women from Boro Park come to Williamsburg for fabric, as if prices were cheaper here, and the ladies from Williamsburg flock to Boro Park as if they will find a *metziah* there."

Faige prepares her answer. "Ma, it's not the *metziah* I'm going for. I just want to get out of the house. I need a break. The idea of taking the baby to Idy is like a dream come true." Idy, Faige's sister-in-law, always manages to fit in day-long emergency trips to Monroe, Monsey, or Lakewood, leaving Faige with a nursing infant who supposedly takes a bottle.

"Ma, a change is good for me. It's not the fabric. It's the break from the baby and household chores that makes one day in Boro Park feel like a two-week vacation in Florida."

In the end, after she'll finish her speech, her mother will say in a caring voice that she'll take Moishele to the doctor so that Faige can still have her treat by going with a friend. "And don't rush home," she'll add. "I'll make sure to have a hot supper ready for the children when they come home."

With tears in her eyes, Faige croaks, "Mommy, why are you doing this for me? I don't deserve it."

"Faige," her mother replies, "I don't deserve arthritis either. We take what Hashem gives us, not what we deserve. Besides, you do deserve it. You are the energy fuse for the entire household. If you don't take care of that one person, who will take care of the seven children and husband?"

"Ma, you're a doll. Do you know that?"

"Well, I'm glad you say that now, because when you were fifteen, you always said that other mothers were better than I was."

"Ma, I was so young then, silly and selfish. You didn't take me seriously, did you?"

"Well, I tried not to, but at times..."

"Ma, I'm sorry. Please remember that I was only a kid then, wrapped up in myself."

"Don't feel too bad, Faige. Hashem has a way of fixing things. He takes revenge on kids, did you know?"

"Really? How?"

"One day, he makes them into parents, too."

Being a Mother Is Hard Work

There is probably no mother who cannot identify with Faige's busy schedule. What infuriated Faige most was the bus driver's comment. How dare he compare raising two children to raising eight, ten, or fourteen? Faige was smart. She let it go and didn't make an argument out of it. But her mother — thank God for her. She understood. Maybe because she herself had been a mother of six little children once upon a time. And she did it when disposable diapers were a luxury mothers didn't dare entertain.

But Faige has plenty of pressures to make up for the luxury of Pampers her mother never had. Whichever way you look at it, mothering is not a simple role; it is a job where the mother needs to wear different hats. These include being a conductor who manages to get seven children off to school every morning, most of the time remembering to send a mitzvah note and two pounds of nosh along. Later the cooking begins. She cooks farina for Chanie's sensitive stomach, makes a peanut butter sandwich for Chaim, since she learned that giving in is better than creating a third world war, and prepares baked chicken, potatoes, and vegetable soup for the older children and her husband. By now Faige can compete with the fanciest, most sought after caterer. As a matter of fact, she often entertains the idea of how great it would be to get paid for all this, but before she can add up her profits, she remembers her other duties.

Her husband's white shirts have to be ironed and starched. Secretly Faige asks Hashem to forgive her for the times when she faked it by neatly folding the shirt and then pressing a hot iron on top of it. Baila's dress is only hand washable, Moishele's pants has mud stains and needs to be soaked for two weeks, and the baby spits up six times after every feeding just to see how long it will take before Faige says, "That's it. I'm not changing you anymore today. I don't care who walks through the door."

Most tutors get paid fifteen to twenty dollars an hour. Faige teaches five different grade levels at a time and has learned the skill of make-believe. She pretends she understands the *Chumash* and *Rashi* eight-year-old Yossele is chanting in a continuous rhythm. At first, it's hard to pull him away from his Lego and get him to review, but once he gets into it, he'll repeat it in his sweet sing-song voice over and over, until three-year-old Miriam shouts, "Close the tape recorder already. I don't need it anymore. I can sing the whole song by myself."

Soon Bubby Greenstein, Faige's mother-in-law, drops by. She finds the baby crawling toward her in haste. As she scoops her up for the you're-my-only-grandchild hug, she notices Chanie's soiled stretchy but says nothing, only offers to take some laundry back with her to do in her house.

Three-year-old Miriam wants attention, too, and begins to sing the entire first chapter of *parashas Bereishis* with *Rashi*. Bubby Greenstein throws conflicting glances of admiration and a look that says, "Are you crazy? Why are you teaching her *Chumash* at this age?"

When the fights break out, Faige is grateful for her self-taught psychology techniques. Secretly she knows she could make peace in the Middle East if only they gave her a chance. The United Nations could make good use of her strategies in cooling tempers. After all, she deals daily with flaring tempers, fist fights, and the commotion of five boys and two girls competing for one person's attention.

Her experience doesn't end there. She has been trained by other experienced mothers how to be the best hairdresser in Manhattan. She cuts her boys' hair like a pro, and her girls never have to go to the hair stylist. She does them all herself.

By the time Faige's made her first bar mitzvah, she has learned to create such fancy cakes they make the bakery cakes look pale and sickly. When she will (with God's help) make her first wedding, she will have become a professional dress designer, sewing all the dresses for the girls and herself. When people ask, "How do you manage it all?" Faige doesn't put on any shows. She merely replies, "I never said I manage. It would be more honest to say I survive!"

You Don't Have to Be Perfect

The truth is that even just surviving is terrific. Many mothers don't do even that. They end up being chronically tired, nervous, and short-tempered so that when the grandchildren come along they are too worn out to enjoy them. The great day they have dreamed of — the day when they can get an uninterrupted eight hours of sleep — has arrived, but they are too nervous to sleep.

They have become conditioned to operate on high speed, and they don't know how to relax. Worse still, their emotional and physical health has been so overstrained they turn to homeopathy, vitamins, and a yeast-free diet and still cannot make peace with themselves so they can relax and enjoy the fruits of their hard labor — their grandchildren. In desperation, many young grandmothers turn to sleeping pills or anti-anxiety medication to ease the effects of chronic stress.

How can one avoid such an unfavorable long-term growth of one's dedication to mothering? Does one have to sacrifice her emotional, mental, and physical well-being in the name of mothering?

Research has proven again and again that this scenario does not have to happen. In all probability, the mother's efforts and dedication are extreme. A mother does not have to be perfect in every way. If the kitchen gets cleaned only once a week, no one will suffer. If the family eats takeout pizza twice a month, the family will survive. And if she can get help, she can even take a nap sometimes to maintain her health.

And most of all, she needs to take out time for herself. If she can't find time to relax, she should steal it. Parenting is probably the toughest business in the world. Taking a respite doesn't cost — it pays dividends to the entire family. By keeping in mind that everything does not have to be perfect, maybe she'll be able to do even more than "survive."

The Absentee Mother

Another extreme, which isn't uncommon either, is where the mother is hardly at home. Leah is just such a person. As soon as the children leave for school, she is off on her own adventures: weekly shopping at Loehmann's, usually on Wednesdays when the new merchandise is displayed, legal holiday expeditions to Woodbury Common to catch the sales — Elizabeth Klein and Laura Ashley designer prices of $550 reduced to $375. On the way back, Leah and her shopping club grab a late lunch and discuss the bargains until suppertime. When Leah arrives home laden with her purchases, she collects the children from three different neighbors. She slaps some salami sandwiches together, floods them with mustard and ketchup, and bribes the kids with half a tub of pareve ice cream for dessert if they eat quickly.

Later, when Shlomie begins to complain about a stomachache and Berel about the fight in yeshivah, Leah begs off. "Please, children, can't you see how tired I am? I can barely keep my head up. My morning headache has taken a turn for the worse. I think I have a migraine. Berel, please give me three extra-strength Tylenols. Shlomie, be a sport. Throw the paper plates in the garbage and play with Yossi for a while. I feel so sorry for him. He was at the babysitter's all day."

Leah collapses into her bed, vowing never to go out again, or at least until the kids have all had their bar mitzvahs. With a deep sense of repentance that washes the guilt away, Leah falls asleep. Her sleep is short-lived, since she forgot to close the ringers.

"Shlomie! Get the phone!"

The phone continues to shrill.

"Berel! Get the phone!"

Silence. No one seems to be home. Leah leaps out of bed, knowing only too well that when the house is too quiet trouble is brewing. She finds all the kids in the backyard playing, oblivious to the phone ringing. Grateful that all is well, she grabs the phone muttering, "Someone knows I'm home, or she would have hung up five minutes ago."

"Hello, Leah? I'm so glad you're home. I have the most marvelous news to tell you."

"Yocheved, can I call you back tomorrow? I'm kind of busy right now."

"Tomorrow? Are you crazy? The membership ends tonight!"

"Membership? What membership?"

"That's what I'm calling you about. Jack La Lanne has a half-price special for their twice-weekly Women's Night, which includes swimming, aerobics, and tennis. The hours are from seven to nine-thirty Monday and Wednesday evenings."

Of course, Leah can't resist. And meanwhile her family suffers.

Neither extreme is healthy. Just as poor parenting, as when a mother puts her children last and friends or job first, results in neglected and disturbed children, so too going to the other extreme of only parenting and not allowing oneself time for relaxation or a little fun results in a mother neglecting her own emotional and physical needs. The best course is to try to find a medium. Of course the family should be the mother's primary concern. But if she takes a break from her twenty-four-hour-a-day job to do something for herself, she will most likely be a better parent for her children after her break. The need to temporarily disengage from the daily chores is not a luxury, but an absolute necessity. On the other hand, if a mother finds herself spending many hours a day away from home so that she is too tired to care for her children, perhaps she needs to reevaluate how she is spending her time and whether she can be there more for her family. No matter how loving a caregiver, or how much fun the kids have at the neighbors', there is no substitute for a mother.

Healthy Friendships Need Healthy Relationships

M iriam spends her summers at a nice *heimishe* bungalow colony. She recites *tehillim* every day after davening. She prides herself on attending weekly *shiurim* and is the first to offer to babysit for anyone in need. Today she was feeling slighted and hurt. Her three neighbors, Bracha, Sima, and Rifkie, had gone out for ice cream in Monticello last night and she was not invited to join them. To add insult to injury, when she had the car just last week, she had invited the same three neighbors to go to Apollo Mall with her.

"How could they have been so callous as to not even tell me about it?" she lamented to everyone she passed on her way to the grocery store. "Whenever I go anywhere, I always let it be known so that others can join me if they wish."

Her pool friend, Chani, trying to help, said, "The truth is that the three of them are all takers. If I come out with a fresh plate of homemade cookies, they smell it immediately and come to taste half a dozen. If Rifkie makes something special like homemade blintzes, she invites only her clique of friends into her bungalow. She wouldn't dare bring it out to the public."

Rachel Leah, seeing the hurt on Miriam's face and the anger on Chani's, offered her philosophical input. "It's best not to expect anything from anyone. It's a selfish world out there. Last year, when I had to go into the city for my first cousin's *levayah*, not one of them had offered to take any of my six children. I had to take the two little ones with me."

Her speech trailed off as she spotted Sima walking toward them with a big smile on her face. Immediately Miriam hurried into the grocery store so as not to meet her face to face. Sima gave Rachel Leah a big hello and blurted out, "I don't know what I would have done if not for Rifkie and Bracha. They saved my life last night. My husband had promised to come out for today and then called to cancel due to an emergency in his company. I was so depressed until Bracha and Rifkie forced me out of the bungalow. In the ice cream store I met my best friend from first grade, and we talked as if we had parted just yesterday. It was wonderful. Today I feel so much better."

She lowered her voice as she continued, "I hope Miriam wasn't upset that she wasn't with us. I had gone into her bungalow to get her, but she wasn't there. I tried the laundry room and several bungalows to find her. In the end, I had to run because it was getting late. If you see her, please tell her I must speak to her. I bought her the biggest ice cream sundae they had to make up for it. It's sitting in my freezer begging to be eaten."

Shamefaced, Rachel Leah muttered a hasty goodbye and went into the grocery. She felt bad, unsure why her conscience was nagging her. What did she do wrong? Why was she feeling bad when she had good news about the ice cream sundae to tell?

She pushed open the screen door. Miriam was still at it. She was telling other buyers about her agonizing disappointment. This time Rachel Leah felt no empathy for Miriam. Instead the dreadful truth filled her heart, and she found it hard to speak. *Lashon hara* is a lot more detrimental than not being invited for an outing. Besides, why didn't anyone try to think of a good reason Miriam was not invited?

The *lashon hara* had to stop. With a shriek, Rachel Leah screamed, "Enough! Enough *lashon hara.*" The store suddenly became so quiet the humming of the freezer sounded deafening. All stood frozen as Rachel Leah said, "There must be a better way of dealing with disappointments and anger than telling everyone about it. There must."

"What am I supposed to do?" rebuked Miriam. "Get a heart attack? Hold it in till I *plotz*? It's a big favor to me to be able to unburden myself. No, it's not *lashon hara*. It's a mitzvah! My psychologist friend claims most physical illness like ulcers, anxieties, and heart attacks come from holding in one's pain. To prevent such calamities, one must speak about his pain."

At that moment, I entered the store and found everyone looking at me. For a moment I felt terribly embarrassed. Did I have my *tichel* on backward? Was I again wearing two different pairs of slippers? As I nervously checked myself, Chani began to speak softly. "Rachel, what is your opinion? If someone is pained, should she speak about what's in her heart to avoid getting a nervous breakdown? What about the issue of *lashon hara*?"

"You're asking a good question," I replied, relieved to find that everything was intact. "There is really no contradiction between psychology and the Torah. They both agree that deep painful emotions inside are unhealthy. How one expresses his pain is where *frumkeit* comes in. One cannot simply spill his sob stories about friends and neighbors to anyone who cares to listen. That is pure *lashon hara*. Don't hide behind the excuse 'I have to get it out of my system' to allow yourself the liberty to talk negatively about your family members, friends, and neighbors. One must be extremely careful when expressing oneself not to transgress the laws of *lashon hara*."

It is a tricky situation. If one is unsure of how to go about bridging the two worlds of avoiding *lashon hara* and not suffering internal pain, it is best to ask a qualified *posek*. I can, however, offer advice on how to avoid having to ventilate to the whole world. It is quite simple. Go directly to the person who has hurt you and tell him or her how you feel. By doing this, you avoid bursting with emotional pain to every bystander and direct it where it belongs — to the person who made you feel that way in the first place. Often you will find there was a misunderstanding and the other person never intended to hurt you.

The Yom Tov Blues

Somewhere along the way, we seemed to have gotten off track. Instead of concentrating on how special and beautiful the *yamim tovim* are, we are busy concentrating on how clean our houses are and who makes the fanciest foods. What if neighbor Chaya walked in and stepped into baby Chaim's crumbled cookie on the floor? Without a doubt the world would fall apart, right?

Consider this common scenario: A neighbor walks into the house and says, "Wow, your house is so clean. How do you manage to keep everything so orderly?" Immediately the hostess replies, "Oh no, my house is really such a mess. I just pushed all the toys under the couch and slapped a fresh tablecloth on the table." By the time the discussion, excuses, and validation of cleanliness is over, the men are coming home from shul.

It is time to review our priorities. No one will go to Heaven for a clean house, certainly not one peppered with yelling and tension from everyone trying to make the house look perfect for *yom tov*. I cannot see how one can do both — keep a spotless house and a spotless mouth and avoid yelling. It has to be one or the other.

I am one of those who have a half-messy house. It makes me feel normal and human. I'd rather feel at peace in a home that is not pristine than anxious about making the perfect *yom tov*. I cringe when I hear everyone comparing notes. Chani makes forty portions of stuffed cabbage, Faige boasts that she has no cleaning lady before *yom tov*, and Chavi assures us that all the food she serves is homemade, including the pickles.

I serve Reisman's cake for breakfast. Instead of baking cakes, I spend time with the children, baking round challos, allowing them to share in the *yom tov* preparations. I ignore the ladies' looks as I happily relate that instead of making cucumber salad I wrote a long letter to my granddaughter upon her second birthday. Though she cannot read, I am sure that when she can she will value it more than a spick-and-span kitchen that boasts of gleaming counters free of fingerprints.

The first day of *yom tov* I allow my daughter to create a Chinese dish for lunch and invite two sisters-in-law and their families for the meal with a request to bring one dish. I know that I am committing the worst sin by using paper plates, but I think God will forgive me quicker for this sin than that of losing my temper due to the pressure of preparing for company. And I have my cleaning lady come *motza'ei yom tov* to clean up so I can spend the time with the children organizing their work and school schedules for the next day instead of ignoring them because I have to clean up the mess left after *yom tov*.

When Chanukah approaches, I am once again faced with decisions. Should I make a party for my family? My friends? My neighbors? My workmates? My country friends? If I do make a party for either group, do I ask them to make a dish or should I do what I did one year? I invited everybody and did all the cooking and preparations myself, refusing offers of help with "Oh, it's no big deal. I just throw this and that into the oven and six dishes come out, ready to be served." To another friend who suggested I use pretty paper goods, I reply with confidence and determination, "I never get to use my fancy cutlery and expensive dishes. When if not now?"

Well, the party was a huge success. I loved the compliments and thank you calls claiming that my party deserved to be placed in the society page of our local paper. The only drawback was that I was laden with guilt for the many days it took my frayed nerves and body to recuperate. Too tired to prepare latkes for the family, we served frozen ones that tasted more like rubber than potatoes. When the children wanted to make doughnuts, I refused to allow them the fun for fear of being asked too many questions my delicate nerves could not handle. Any energy I had on reserve was saved for clients at work. I felt like a fraud counseling mothers on setting priorities between family, work friends, and social competition when I myself had goofed so badly.

Probably I will make a party on Chanukah. But I will use paper goods, buy some food, accept any offers of help, and limit the amount of people to a number I can easily handle. And, most important, I will find time to play dreidel and bake doughnuts filled more with love than jam with the children. We will make latkes with potatoes peeled by kids and shared with adults. And if the kitchen is a mess, I'll just ask my cleaning lady to stay longer.

The Luckiest Person
in the World

I GUESS logic moves out when emotions move in. I learned this lesson in February 1986, when I took in two little girls to live with us. I skillfully rationalized my decision with persuasive facts. I wasn't a social worker yet, so the rules of not taking a patient home didn't apply to me, not yet. As a matter of fact, I was only an undergraduate social work student apprenticing at a girl's yeshivah elementary school once a week. Besides, I was facing a difficult dilemma and needed a solution — fast.

Five-year-old Dina and her seven-year-old sister, Shani, had no home to go to after school. Once again their mother had been hospitalized at Paine Whitney Psychiatric Center due to a new bout of panic attacks. It was fruitless to call their father in Israel. Their parents had divorced three years ago, and Mr. Friedman had successfully relocated and remarried a young woman over there. While he couldn't hide the fact that he had two children, he thought the less he had to do with them the better.

While many people are able to control severe panic

attacks with medication, Mrs. Friedman claimed she could not. At first I believed her and sincerely empathized with her, but soon I realized that she had omitted an important piece of information, which Dina filled in during one of our play therapy sessions. "You know," she said, "my mother is smarter than the doctors. As soon as she feels a bit better, she stops taking her medication. She throws it out or flushes it down the toilet, saying she is fine now. 'There is no need to take it when I am fine,' she says. The doctors tell her that this is not true, but she says that doctors are money hungry and want to keep people on medicine so they can get rich off them."

After a couple of good weeks, Mrs. Friedman always regressed and began a new cycle of panic attacks. As her behavior spun out of control she was hospitalized, where she again found relief with medication. This morning was such a day. The fear of dying overwhelmed her again, and she was reacting in her usual manner, running from door to door in her apartment building, shrieking hysterically for someone to help her. With blazing eyes and a wild look of terror that forced trickles of perspiration to stream down her face, she would scream uncontrollably, "Why aren't you helping me? Can't you see that I am dying? I'm dying right in front of your eyes! Why aren't you calling Hatzalah?"

The adults in the building were accustomed to her panic attacks and took them in stride, consoling her, "Don't worry, Mrs. Friedman, you know you won't die. You never do. You only feel that way." Some would even invite her in and soothe her with a cup of coffee and more kind words. Others, especially the children, would get so frightened they would run shrieking upon seeing her in the elevator or in the hallway, even on days when she was perfectly fine. And she had many fine days.

Some days were better than others, especially when someone in the apartment building was making a *simchah*. Whether Mrs. Friedman was invited or not, she would present the neighbor with the fanciest homemade cake made from scratch. Whenever someone needed a candy mold, chocolate, or confectioners' sugar, they knocked on Mrs. Friedman's door. Mrs. Friedman would always throw in extra items you didn't even ask for. "You must take this," she would insist. "This way I'll feel like I partook in the baking of your challos or Shabbos cake."

Unfortunately, her good periods were getting shorter, and her panic attacks were becoming more frequent. On those days her elderly mother would come to the rescue and take the two children to live with her and her husband in their one-bedroom apartment in Williamsburg. Recently, however, she was diagnosed with Alzheimer's disease. While she functioned most days, she found it increasingly difficult to care for her grandchildren. To help out, Zeide would fill in, in spite of the fact that the left side of his face and left hand had been paralyzed since World War II. Lately his heart was giving him trouble, but he decided to keep the chest pains to himself so he could be available for the grandchildren.

It was two o'clock in the afternoon when Paine Whitney informed me that Mrs. Friedman had been hospitalized once again. I immediately contacted the grandparents, but was unable to reach them. I was nervous. Where could the children go? I looked up their emergency number on file. The name written next to the number was Amy Steinmetz, but both children insisted they had never heard of her. I called her anyway.

Yes, she had heard about the Friedman children and would take them in temporarily. She explained that she was a first cousin to Mrs. Friedman, lived in Staten Island with two cats, one dog, and a parakeet, but had plenty of room for the children, too. No, she didn't have children, since she had never married, but she felt confident she could care for her cousin's darling children.

The minute I hung up I felt a flush of panic sweep over me like a tidal wave. Two cats, a dog, and a parakeet? And the children didn't even know her. With a false sense of enthusiasm, I told the children that Amy Steinmetz was their cousin from Staten Island and she was on her way over to take them to her house. Little Dina pretended not to hear me. The only indication of acknowledgment was a puddle that began to form on the floor. I knew from previous experience that whenever she was very scared or nervous she would lose control of her bladder. Her older sister was more sophisticated. With the authoritative voice of a policewoman she blurted out, "I'm not going to Amy Steinmetz. She is a strange lady with a lot of dogs and cats. I'd rather sleep in school."

At four o'clock, after a dozen calls to neighbors and distant relatives, there was still no home where the Friedman children could go. Their grandparents were not home either. I had two choices left — either to call Ohel Children's Home and Family Services or the police, who would place the children in temporary homes. Glancing in the direction of the two children who had been huddling together since two o'clock, I couldn't contain the pain in my heart. Never had I seen such a pitiful scene.

Shani was wiping up her little sister's puddle with

paper towels and whispering to her in a voice loud enough to reach my desk. She glanced at me to make sure I was listening. "Don't worry," she said, hugging her sister tightly. "Mrs. Schmidt won't leave us here. She will do something for us, just wait and see. She might even take us to her house."

My ears perked up. I couldn't believe what I had just heard. Shani had figured it out.

"Listen, Dina, we can promise to be good and helpful. We will tell her that we even do dishes and clean better than a cleaning lady."

That was it. I could take it no longer. I burst into the principal's office and said I would take them home for the night until the grandparents could be reached tomorrow. Rabbi Levi, the principal, must have been relieved because he said it was a good solution.

As I ushered the children out of the building relieved that they had a place to go and would not have to fear the unknown, the principal called after me, "Mrs. Schmidt, what kind of therapy would you call this?"

I asked what he thought it was. He replied with a warm smile. "Jewish therapy, no?"

Little did I know that the Jewish therapy would last three long winter months. The grandparents were not home the next day either. A call to Beth Israel Medical Center confirmed that they had both been hospitalized yesterday morning. Bubby was found wandering the streets, unable to remember her name and address, and Zeide had had a mild heart attack. Again I entertained thoughts of calling the police or Ohel, but I didn't. Some relative would surely come to fetch them soon, and besides, a call had been placed to their father in Jerusalem.

All day I waited for the long-distance call to come through and give me further instructions. I shouted at anyone who dared to use the phone, even for a minute.

By one o'clock, I realized that with Shabbos approaching shortly, I had better keep them as guests for "just one Shabbos." There was an uncomfortable gnawing feeling that I was getting more than I bargained for, but I pushed it aside when I saw how excited the children were to be invited to stay until after Shabbos.

Dina doubled up with my own five-year-old daughter, and Shani slept on the high-riser next to my ten-year-old daughter. My two boys shared the other bedroom and were glad not to be disturbed by two children who alternated between "loving" and "hating" being in a strange home. Dina kept whimpering, "When is Mommy coming home? I want Mommy."

Shani was more mature and motherly. She explained that they should be grateful that Mrs. Schmidt had taken them in until their mother got better. She pointed out that here no one screamed — at least, no one had since they arrived yesterday. Finally Dina couldn't resist any longer and asked my Sara quietly, "When is the screaming going to start already? I can't wait anymore. I want to get it over with so I can relax already."

Sara was cute. She answered to the point. "My mother hardly yells, but she sure punishes a lot. If I don't listen, I have to go up to my room for ten minutes."

Little Dina went further with her inquisition. "How come you are so rich?"

"We're not rich. Each month my father worries about paying the mortgage, and Mommy always gives him a look to stop talking like that in front of us."

"But you have toys," insisted Dina. "You must be rich."

"Doesn't everyone have toys? What am I supposed to play with if I don't have any dolls?"

"Well," began Dina, beginning to whine and twirl her black hair, "I don't even have one doll. My mother doesn't let me have a single toy, not even crayons. I must leave my crayons at school every day. She says they create a mess and she has no head for such silly things."

"What about birthdays, Chanukah, and special occasions? Don't your *bubby* and *zeidy* buy you anything?"

"Yes, they do. Once they even bought me a Barbie doll, but my mother took it away. Like I said before, she can't handle mess. She says it gives her panic attacks."

It didn't take long for Sara to find out what panic attacks were. I almost had my first one a half-hour after their conversation. On impulse, I decided to check Dina's head for nits. The twirling of her hair had accelerated to scratching, and I got a bit nervous. Just to make sure, I parted her hair in half and gasped for air, screaming. About a dozen little bugs began to buzz around Dina's head, and she barely noticed. Nor did she react to my screeching. I guess it was nothing new to her. Sara ran out screaming to her older brother, "Hurry, call Hatzalah. Mommy made bugs come out of Dina's head."

Fortunately my son checked the gravity of the situation before he called. Quickly I told him to run to the drugstore for Quell, while I hysterically stripped the linen.

Four hours later, the linen, which had been washed with three cups of Tide, bleached, and disinfected with a bottle of Quell, was put back on the bed. Dina was cozy with a towel wrapped turban-style around her head.

I wish I could end the story here, but unfortunately there was more, a lot more, to follow. First of all, there was still no one to take the children. My husband and I decided to hold on to the children until their mother got better and was stabilized and discharged. Usually that happened within a week a so. What we didn't realize was that Mrs. Friedman, who had been administered an experimental drug to be given by injection once a month by her physician, had to be observed around the clock for the next two months in four-week intervals.

On the bright side, I got firsthand experience on how neglected children view the world. On the other hand, I almost went crazy from the learning experience and could have easily done with less education. Today, when I look back, I'm glad I can put my experience to good use.

I can better empathize with the little clients who come to my office, and I also appreciate and value myself as a parent. I forgive myself more easily when I am not the great mother I would like to be. I realize that as long as the home is stable most of the time, occasional bouts of chaos don't have a significant effect on the growing child. When, however, the home is in crises most of the time, as that of the Friedman children, certain emotional neuroses manifest and threaten the long-term stability of children. If their neuroses remain unaddressed and their environment does not improve, their chances of living a healthy adult life are slim. Children cannot learn a normal healthy lifestyle on their own. It has to be taught to them by their parents or significant others in their lives. If they receive no view other than the one they are exposed to, they more often than not repeat the very same lives they hated so much.

With deep commitment, I plunged into being a surrogate mother for these two deprived children. In my zeal to make up for their lost childhood, I consciously attempted to give them megadoses of love. Much to my amazement, I found that they were not always as eager to receive my love as I was to give it. As a matter of fact, it often made them nervous.

During dinner, Shani noticed who needed a spoon, fork, cup, or salt. Without being asked, she leaped up to give the family member the missing utensil. I felt sorry for Shani's need to take over and told her it was okay for her to sit and concentrate on her own needs. I would help anyone who needed assistance.

This was easier said than done. Shani could not sit still and enjoy her meal. The more I asked her to relax and look after only her needs, the more jumpy and nervous she got. Then it struck me like a bolt of lightning — Shani had been trained to be a caretaker almost her entire seven years of life. It was the role she was accustomed to and comfortable with regardless of the consequences it created in the disruption of her own dinner. Telling her not to disrupted her customary role and made her feel even more frustrated and unhappy than interrupting her meal every minute.

Putting Shani to bed proved to be another lesson of confusion. The first night she cried herself to sleep. Each time I approached her and offered to hold her or listen to her tell me what was bothering her, she would cry even louder. I finally took the hint. I left her alone to let her feel sorry for herself in private. Two hours and twenty minutes later she was finally asleep, but not peacefully.

Every few minutes her body would convulse with a huge sigh that turned into a whimpering cry.

The next day I decided I would not force my care onto the children. When I put Shani to sleep, I didn't asked her if she wanted to give me a good-night hug. I said Shema with her, kissed my own five-year-old good night, and hastily made my exit, not wanting to slip up again. But Shani's shriek stopped me cold in my tracks before I had even closed the door to their room. I couldn't believe what I was hearing. "Mrs. Schmidt, you don't love me! You don't care about me! You hate me. Everyone hates me. That's why they don't hug me."

I braced myself, saying, "Shani, would you like me to give you a hug?"

Without another word, Shani leaped into my arms and crushed me with all her might. I remember the thought that crossed my mind: *She doesn't even know how to give me a hug without choking me.*

For the next hour and a half, I sat in the rocking chair holding and rocking her softly. The minute she sensed I was attempting to get up and put her into her bed, she would spring up with wide-open eyes and beg me to hold her some more.

As days turned into weeks, I became more and more aware of the importance of stability, love, and positive discipline. I had taken so much for granted until now. Receiving a call from school that my child had a fever seemed so minor compared to receiving a call from the doctor that Dina had pinworms and impetigo. Having my ten-year-old fail her spelling test was a pleasure compared to the anxiety Shani put us all through aiming for a hundred on her math test.

Being a good student was of the utmost importance to Shani, and she stopped at nothing to do her best. She studied history and spelling by herself with the intensity of a *sofer* writing a *sefer Torah*. If she got stuck and forgot a word, she would pinch her hand in exasperation and hiss, "*Oish, oish,* I must get it right! I'm so stupid!" Later, in bed, she couldn't fall asleep because she was worried about page 87 which she was still unsure about. Again and again she sprang from her bed to check page 87, then page 101, then page 99...

My heart ached for these children, and I found there was little I could do to help them with their neuroses, which interfered not only with their lives, but the structure of our entire family as well. There was a family party to which both adults and children were invited. Of course, we intended to have Dina and Shani accompany us, but they had other plans. When Sara told Dina the exciting news that we were all going to Bubby's house for a *melaveh malkah*, Dina had a fit. Hysterical tears accompanied the dripping puddle that appeared on the floor. Naturally, being the spokesperson, Shani understood and explained Dina's dilemma to us. Dina was frightened of strangers, especially when there were many of them in one place.

Poor Shani. She desperately wanted to attend the party, but quickly offered to sacrifice her fun by staying home to babysit for Dina. This was out of the question, since Shani herself was only seven years old. There was no way I could leave two small children alone. Shani kept reassuring me that it was okay. "At home, Mommy always left me to babysit, even when I was in Pre-1A. Now that I'm in the second grade, I'm not even afraid anymore. If I hear a noise, I just put my head under the covers and say *tehillim*, and the noise always goes away."

In the end, we compromised by taking turns. I went with the children for half the time, and my husband went for the other half.

The days moved slowly for us all. Silently we were counting the weeks and then the days when their mother would be discharged. Dina and Shani, however, had other plans. They decided to get adopted into our family. They did this by refusing to speak to their mother on the phone, telling neighbors that we had decided to adopt them, and writing "Schmidt" instead of "Friedman" on their homework and tests.

At first I was furious, but later my fury led to fear. How in the world would I tell them that their mother was finally coming home next week? The mere mention of their mother would create another puddle on the floor by Dina and a bout of scratching that Shani was unable to cease. When she was desperate, she would bite her hands and claim that biting helped stop her from scratching.

In spite of these symptoms, I spoke to them in a cool, calm voice yet with internal anxiety. "Children, I spoke to your mother today. She sounds wonderful. It seems the new drug is more effective than the doctors anticipated. She is so happy to be coming home. She promised to bake cupcakes with you both the minute she walks through the door."

No response. My words fell on deaf ears.

Finally, the eight weeks of unbroken tension, daily drama, exhausting work, and tons of patience were coming to a close. Soon we would be a normal family again. The morning I packed their belongings into the trunk of the car and drove them to school where their mother was waiting to meet them was the worst morning of my life. As their mother entered the room, both children clung to me like two drowning people hanging on to a rope.

"Dina, give Mommy a hug. Shani, come, let me see how much you have grown," said their mother.

Silence. No response. They clutched my blouse even tighter. The children refused to budge. I finally had to call for assistance. The secretary, principal, and teachers were all wrestling with the children in an attempt to break their hold. By this time, I had lost my composure. I was crying louder than the children, not understanding why I was crying. Isn't this what I had wanted from the very start? I was their temporary mother. I had never intended to replace their real mother. Why, then, was my heart breaking in two? Thankfully the staff managed to loosen Dina's grip and, soon after, Shani's.

The second I was free, I ran from the office as if the building were on fire. I didn't look back, not even once. I headed straight for my car and drove off. When my vision got too blurred from crying, I would stop at the curb until I regained my composure and drive on. Soon I reached home. Luckily no one was in the house, and I was able to mourn my loss of dignity in privacy.

I wish I could say that soon things went back to normal. They didn't. My children missed Dina and Shani in spite of their frequent bickering. They claimed the house was too quiet, too dull. They complained that they had to get up from the table to get their own salt, spoons, and napkins. And so we grieved and mourned much longer than I ever would have imagined. At the next family *melaveh malkah*, I looked at my watch nervously to see if it was my turn to go home to babysit Dina, only to realize that it was no longer necessary. For no reason, I found myself wiping tears off my face that had no business being there. I was happy for them, wasn't I? Their mother was so much better. Isn't this what I really wanted?

Suddenly I wasn't so sure. In my heart of hearts, I finally admitted to myself what I did not want to admit. I had grown to love those children, and that part of me did not want to let them go.

Two months later, the school was in the midst of presenting their annual Purim play. Each year a different grade performed the Purim finale. As always, I would look in for a few minutes of the play just to show my face to the children I was counseling and who had invited me to watch them perform. As I entered the large auditorium, I heard a familiar voice singing a solo. I looked up, and there was Shani, beautifully costumed as Queen Esther — the leading role in the play. My heart skipped a beat as I watched, first in shock and then in awe. Her poise, her confidence, her performance, were superb. No one would ever guess she had such wrenching internal issues. As she gracefully danced on the stage, I had a sudden thought.

No, Shani, you are not acting. This is real. To pretend to have the confidence and charm of a queen takes great confidence. You are not acting. This is you. You are a real Queen Esther.

The stone in my heart lifted, and I finally let go of my loss. For the first time since they had left, I felt whole and healed. I was finally able to see their stay at my house as a positive event for all of us. I began to recount the many positive things Dina and Shani had learned and taken home with them, as well as the many things my family had learned from these two young girls. We learned to appreciate what we had instead of griping about what we didn't have. I realized the enormous role we, as parents, play in the emotional health of our children. Our input is immeasurable. How special this job is. How special we mothers must be that Hashem entrusted us with this great responsibility.

I left the auditorium with Shani's voice ringing in my ears. And I was left wondering: who gained more from their stay? At first I thought Dina and Shani had gained the most from the structure and nurturing. Then I thought it was my children, who had gained the experience of sharing and appreciation. In the end, I decided it was I who had gained the most. My role as a mother had been validated more than ever. I suddenly felt like the luckiest person in the world.

Middle Adulthood

Productivity versus Stagnation

The tree of self has grown significantly. The birth and maturity of its many branches have blossomed fresh leaves, offering the promise of future branches.

How a woman divides her time is the challenge of this time of life. It is also a measure of her emotional health. The giving of one's self to extended family is powerfully gratifying. Yet, if one is to maintain emotional health boundaries must be set. The person in mid-adulthood must also find time for personal rejuvenation.

A forty-year-old attains understanding,
a fifty-year-old can offer counsel,
a sixty-year-old attains seniority...

— Rabbi Yehudah ben Teima, Avos

The Sandwich Generation

By the time adults reach middle age, from forty to sixty years old, they are more settled on the journey of life. They are less likely to be searching and struggling for identification, careers, and family fulfillment. These issues have been resolved or settled, for better or worse. Acceptance of both successes and failures of life's expectations leads to a more mature internal self. Adults begin to appreciate, more than before, simple things in life. A clear day devoid of clouds brings a song of serenity to the heart.

Ailing Parents

As the importance of pleasing others recedes, another challenge often emerges at this stage of life. One's own parents, who once were a source of emotional and physical support, now begin to show signs of aging. Many illnesses, such as diabetes, Alzheimer's, cancer, colitis, ulcers, strokes, and heart attacks, necessitate long-term care from children who are still in the midst of raising their own large families. Much as parents would like to avoid turning to their busy children, they often have no choice.

Usually it is the daughters that parents turn to, because

they are often more sensitive and willing to sacrifice than the sons. This is not to say that sons don't help their ailing parents. They definitely do. However, statistics overwhelmingly prove that daughters are more likely than sons to sacrifice their time and that they have greater patience for elderly parents. The cliché "A son is a son till he gets a wife; a daughter is a daughter all her life!" makes the point clearly. However, within the Orthodox community, statistics do not always apply. it is just as common to see sons taking ailing parents to doctors and caring for them.

The challenges fall harder on women because they are caring for young children, supporting married children, being housekeepers, shoppers, and cooks for the family, and even working outside the home. When a woman's mother suddenly falls and needs surgery, the woman joins the ranks of the sandwich generation. She runs from cooking meatballs and spaghetti and serving it to the little ones to cooking boiled chicken without salt and running to the hospital to serve it to her mother. While the mental and physical strain is enormous, knowing that no job in the world is more prestigious and commendable reaps internal satisfaction and boundless rewards.

Being an Older Mother

Older mothers are often different from their younger counterparts. When we're in our twenties, bearing healthy children seems almost taken for granted. In mid-life, appreciation for the health of the newborn is more intensely felt.

The older mother has a larger store of patience. Behavior that was once a nuisance is now viewed with humor. Mothers who raised their first children in a cookie mold with rigid demands are generally more lenient with their younger children. Milestones of maturity such as being toilet-trained are met with patience rather than pressure for both child and mother. Children's complaints are taken in stride, not as a personal attack triggering maternal insecurities. Parents in general are more relaxed about the challenges of child-rearing and feel less threatened by childhood issues and personalities. What years ago seemed threatening appears today amicable and safe. Showing off and impressing others has become secondary if not nonexistent. Personal health and emotional equilibrium take a front seat.

My Children Are Married, but I'm Busier than Ever

At mature adulthood, some of the children are, *baruch Hashem*, happily married with children of their own. Grandmothers naturally relish visits from their married children and *eineklech*. But a dilemma begins to emerge like black spots on a once healthy red apple when married children go beyond a nice visit to give the grandparents a chance to *shep nachas*. They pack up the children, bottles, clothes, and diapers and move in to their parents' home for *yamim tovim* and Shabbosos on a regular basis. There is nothing wrong with this setup if the married children share the chores. When this is the case, both parties, married children and grandparents, reap the rewards of mutual *nachas*, companionship, and a loving relationship.

Why, then, do so many mothers of married children feel exploited by their own beloved children? This occurs when chores are lopsided, leaving grandmother with all the responsibilities, while the married children bask in the freedom of a free vacation. At this point, the experience is no longer a healthy or desirable one. Grandparents put on fake smiles but are too embarrassed to address the issue of shared responsibilities. Children ignore hints or perhaps never even receive them.

Grandparents need to remember that words that are not expressed verbally are not heard. They need to be honest about their feelings. If they are unable to do so, they cannot put the blame on the children. Their inability to relate honestly and clearly is the main issue. Children who overstay or take advantage are the secondary problem. It is no wonder that grandparents turn to friends, neighbors, and siblings with their complaints. Often the built-up frustration explodes at the end of a strained holiday. Like a bad aftertaste, both generations are left feeling miserable and misunderstood.

This typical scenario shuts the door on a healthy relationship till the next *yom tov* rolls around. Mother's maternal need to mend last holiday's conflict feeds well into the need of the married children, who once again desperately want a respite. The urgent compulsion toward peace from both parties necessitates a quick reconciliation.

The cycle turns again...

To make holidays beneficial to all, married children must be sensitive to cues from parents for help. They must try to understand the reasons for their parents' double message. They love to be with their children but are not able to handle the heavy demands of the visit.

Grandmother may be torn apart. She loves her married children but cannot handle the pressure. She puts more food on her plate than she can possibly eat. Doing a solo job is impractical and unrealistic. Having several married children all wanting to take a vacation turns the fairy tale into a nightmare. The preparations of *yom tov*, shopping, cleaning, and cooking in amounts large enough to compete with catering halls creates a human pressure cooker. At any moment, usually toward curtain-closing time, the bomb of resentment explodes into a third world war between married children and their parents. Grandmothers end up crying, grandfathers lose their temper, and children promise never to step foot into the house again.

Children need to shake off the slumber of sleep, to wake up and smell the coffee. Their mother cannot enjoy being with her extended family if she's doing all the work herself. Instead of rejoicing and spending time with the grandchildren, she is nursing a migraine or falling into an exhausted sleep. When *yom tov* is finally over, *she* needs a vacation to recover from the emotional and physical stress of *yom tov*.

Having other unmarried children makes the dilemma easier and more difficult at the same time. Unmarried children can be a great source of help — if they are old enough and willing. The siblings may be young children who cannot help. On the contrary, they may still need their mother to meet their emotional and physical needs. In short, both the young and the older children are competing for their mother's love, nurturing, and attention.

There is a solution to making the three-generation relationship beneficial to all parties involved. Children should not come empty-handed even for one Shabbos. Always bring a gift or token, large or small, depending on your budget. Insist, not offer, to help in the preparation of *yom tov*. Be careful not to become an absentee parent, leaving child-raising to your mother. She has already done her job.

Life is a constant turn of stages and events. While parents may have raised some of their children to adulthood, their work of parenting has not ended under the *chuppah*. There exists a new challenge in life: communicating honestly with their married children. Parents must share in the responsibility of creating a happy reunion when their married children come home. They cannot expect the children to read their minds or perceive their level of physical energy. They have to take extra effort not to be intimidated by their children. They cannot refuse offers of help and say, "Oh, it's really not necessary" — and then fall apart. They must honestly and clearly communicate their physical, emotional, and financial strain to all married guests. Asking the children to pitch in does not make you inadequate grandparents.

Finally, no good comes out of overdoing the cooking preparations. Most of your emotional and physical energy should be reserved for relaxing and playing with the grandchildren.

When parents clearly communicate with their children the importance of sharing the preparations of the holidays, the disadvantages of coming home disappear. Happiness, excitement, and *nachas* reign over the entire family. If children want to feel like they're in a five-star hotel, let them create it. Better yet, let parents and married children take turns. If mother had the children over last *yom tov*, switch roles. This time, parents can visit their children for a much needed change and rest.

When Married Children Move Away

I hear conflicting opinions. My children got married and moved to Israel. My son is in *kollel*, my daughter-in-law just gave birth to the second baby, and the rest of the family is here in America. Some people pity us for not having the *nachas* of the grandchildren close by, while others applaud our courage and strength in allowing them independence. I never know which opinion I'll hear, so I have to be ready with answers for both. To the first group of friends and neighbors, who are busy showing off their *eineklech*, I say, "You are right. I don't know how I ever consented to such self-infliction. But much as I cry over missing them, I don't regret my decision. I support them in living where they feel it is best for them." They give me looks of pity and shake their heads.

To the second group, who look at my strength to let go with awe, I respond, "It's not as easy as it looks. Believe me, I spend many hours crying over the pictures that adorn my living-room table and walls, at the cute four-month-old face pasted onto the kitchen clock." They, too, look at me strangely, not understanding why I'm putting up such a brave front when I hurt so much inside.

It is a very sensitive issue, whether or not to allow young married couples to move across the sea from their parents. But one has to ask, whose decision is it anyway? Do the young married children, merely teenagers, have the right to demand that they be supported in a faraway land? Do parents continue to rule the destiny of married children the same way as unmarried children? Who exactly has the right to decide? The kids or the parents?

The answer depends on how parents view their children. Are these children an extension of themselves, obligated to live as close as possible? Or are they gifts from Hashem, given to parents to raise until adulthood? When they marry, they aren't abandoning their parents — their parents never owned them to begin with. On the contrary, parents have finished their major role in raising, guiding, and nurturing them. Now they are ready to repeat the same pattern of Jewish parenting for the next generation of children, who will be loved dearly and eventually permitted to spread their wings when they grow up and marry.

Yes, letting go is painful. It can take your breath away, leaving you weak as you gasp for strength to plunder on. On the other hand, never letting go is unhealthy to the well-being of the married couple. For them to bond with one another, they need space from parents and family. To build a close relationship with each other, they need to lean on one another rather than on their parents as they are accustomed to doing. To reach their potential and achieve their life goal, be it learning, business, or teaching, they need to be in an environment that is conducive and nurturing to *them*, not to their parents.

This is not to say that children who live near parents cannot gain intimacy with each other or fulfillment. They certainly can. However, it is up to the married children, not the parents, to decide which lifestyle is most fulfilling for them. If Israel is the place that tugs their hearts, parents must not stand in the way. If they are emotionally healthy, they will bear the pain of separation for the sake of the children's happiness. To anyone who asks, "Don't you love them? How can you let them go?" I have one answer: "Yes, of course I love them. That is why I let them go."

A Frum Woman Addicted?

HOW IN the world does an average Boro Park housewife with healthy children, a husband who makes a decent living, and loads of friends suddenly get addicted to Tylenol?

Tylenol? But that's harmless! Doctors even allow pregnant and nursing mothers take it for aches and pains.

True, but Tylenol, like any drug, can become addictive if taken over a long period of time on a steady basis. Too bad my client Mrs. B. didn't know this important fact years ago. She could have saved herself a lot of grief, pain, and six weeks of detoxification in a rehabilitation clinic.

As she told me her story, I became alarmed, thinking how easily people can get into deep trouble with over-the-counter drugs. Her story brought a cold chill down my spine, and I wrapped my sweater around me tightly. I hoped she hadn't noticed. I was embarrassed to feel so caught up in her pain. Being a *frum* woman myself, I wondered if I wasn't overidentifying with her. As a social worker, I should be used to tragic stories and be able to maintain a distance.

But logic doesn't always dominate emotion. The knowledge that she was the only *heimishe* woman in a ward of recovering drug addicts filled me with horror. I imagined them with their comatose stares, erupting without warning into verbal or violent rage. I heard their desperate plea for help go unanswered for hours on end as they lay helplessly thrashing in their straightjackets, and I shuddered in horror.

Mrs. B. needed several sessions before she could articulate her entire shameful experience. For weeks she was too embarrassed to make eye contact with me. I assured her that I did not think less of her because of her experience. I validated her strength in going for proper help and called her a heroine. She smiled meekly, but continued to keep her coat on in shameful silence. A cliché, "Absence of knowledge often harms more than knowledge itself," crossed my mind as I waited impatiently for her to speak.

I said nothing to break her silence. She was given the freedom of choosing the appropriate time for her emotional release. Several times she coughed, as if to prepare herself. Other times she opened her mouth to begin, but she stopped before the words flowed out. I had to use all of my professional training to control my inner impulse to cry, "Get it out! I'm dying to know what happened." Instead, I gently reminded her again and again that telling her story would help her deal with her pain, but only when she felt safe and ready.

Experience taught me that owning a horrendous secret creates a sense of isolation. My role was to listen to her story and mirror her experience nonverbally so that she could regain her emotional equilibrium and return to a normal pattern of life.

Therapy often means remaining silent, waiting for the client to open up. Interestingly, her silent verbal introversion did not hold back the aura of deep shame. It filled the room like smoke. Silently witnessing her emotions and remaining nonjudgmental was my job right now.

My perseverance finally paid off. One day Mrs. B. walked into my office, her steps a bit more brisk than before. Her coat in hand, and she darted a look in my direction, attempting eye contact. Immediately I knew that today's session would be different. She was ready. I thanked Hashem for giving me the patience to wait until the right time. Mrs. B took a deep breath and began.

"About a year ago, my oldest child got engaged. All went well until my mother suffered a heart attack two months before the wedding. I was pulled apart like a rubber band stretched at both ends. I desperately wanted to spend all day and night with my mother, but at the same time I had a million errands to take care of for the wedding. The pressure of both responsibilities threw me into a continuous emotional cyclone. When I was shopping, I wished I was with my mother. When I was with my mother, I remembered lists of things that were left undone. My head began to ache as if a hammer was hitting it. Each day it picked up painful momentum until it became one long chronic migraine."

She stopped talking, and I was afraid she had lost her courage, but she merely blew her nose and continued on. "I started out by taking two Extra-Strength Tylenol every four hours. After three weeks it just wasn't doing the same job. I still had six weeks to go until the wedding and couldn't afford headaches. I upped my dosage to three Extra-Strength Tylenol every four hours, and it worked. Vaguely I became aware that I was consuming more Tylenol than food but rationalized that this was a temporary situation. After the wedding, I would go back to eating regular food."

I asked how many Tylenols she had been taking daily. She promptly took out her pocket calculator and came up with about twelve Extra-Strength Tylenols per day. I gasped. Didn't she know that too much Tylenol could lead to kidney disease? Wasn't it common knowledge that over-the-counter painkiller can cause rebound headaches, often leading to addiction? Apparently not.

It wasn't until my thoughts drifted back to Mrs. B. that I noticed she had stopped speaking. Expressing her pain and fatigue from talking had left her panting breathlessly.

"You don't have to finish the entire story in one day," I reminded her gently, denying my urge to push her on.

Mrs. B. smiled weakly and said, "Thank you for caring. It feels so good to hear someone take an interest in me after being the one to always care for everyone else." Huge tears of gratitude streamed down her hollow cheeks.

Mrs. B. struggled. Perhaps she was afraid she'd lose her courage by the next session and her painful story would be left unfinished. She turned the topic briefly to the emotional issues of her mother, who had passed away. "I hope I was good enough to her. I hope she knew how much I loved her and how sorry I was for the times I made her upset."

Mrs. B. had moved from the painful experience of Tylenol addiction. She now needed to mourn her mother, and I wasn't about to interfere. After ten minutes of sobbing into half a box of tissues she abruptly stopped speaking about her mother and switched the topic to the Shabbos *aufruf*.

"Luckily my mother's condition improved significantly

the week before the *aufruf*, and I was able to give my entire attention to making the arrangements for the twenty couples who flew in for the *simchah*. The *aufruf* was on a Thanksgiving weekend, so relatives made a long weekend out of it. They came in on Thursday for the Monday wedding. I didn't mind really. Neighbors were only too happy to offer their basements and extra bedrooms. But I had to make sure that Aunt Tilly wasn't seated next to Aunt Shaindy, whom she hasn't spoken to for seventeen years. Uncle Raphael smoked and snored. He needed a basement all to himself while his wife kept getting in my way trying to help out. I had consumed an economy-size Tylenol by the time the weekend was over.

"On the day of the wedding, I ran to the drugstore and stocked up on four different painkillers. By that time I was popping two different extra-strength medications, just to be sure. Not wanting to shlep the bottle around with me, I slipped four Tylenol tablets into my shoe, making one shoe tighter than the other. I ignored the discomfort. In the meantime, I put three Excedrins in my mouth, just for extra security. I vaguely remember thinking that my stomach was too queasy to hold any food all day, and for one fleeting moment I wondered if I was giving myself an ulcer. But I was too busy to worry for more than a second. I knew that it was aspirin, not Tylenol, that caused ulcers. Tylenol was totally safe. Besides, the photographers were waiting.

"During the *chuppah*, I cried my eyes out in spite of the fact that I had promised my son I wouldn't shed a tear. It was his wedding, and I was going to abide by his wishes. But making promises before the *chuppah* was easy. During the *chuppah*, I cried unabashedly. I worried that he didn't have everything he needed. Why hadn't I sent toothpaste and soap to the apartment?

"Yes, these are silly things to cry over. Why didn't I think of thanking Hashem for reaching this milestone in my son's life? I'm still not sure. Maybe I was too drugged from the over-the-counter analgesics. What I do remember clearly is that a new pounding headache had began to travel down to my neck and spine. And I was stuck. With the entire crowd watching, how could I possibly reach down to remove the Tylenol from my shoe? Besides, I had nothing to drink and certainly couldn't steal a sip from the Kiddush cup. I had no way of alleviating the pain that was going to be a whopper by the time the *chuppah*, kissing, hugging, and *mazel tovs* were over. I could not wait to run to the groom's room for my next dose of...whatever.

"In great panic, I forgot about the *chasan*'s big day. I forgot to ask Hashem to give him a long happy life with his *kallah*. I forgot to ask for healthy grandchildren or *nachas*. Instead, I cried and prayed that I hadn't forgotten to put the Tylenol in my shoe. I was suddenly so confused, I couldn't remember whether I had or hadn't. I tried concentrating on my feet to see if there was a difference in the shoe size, but it was a useless effort. Both my legs were hurting so badly, and all I felt was searing heat shooting up both legs.

"My confusion frightened me. Was I losing my mind? Hysteria spread a blanket of anxiety over me. I began to shake. I wished the *chuppah* would be over and prayed that I had enough medicine in the groom's room. As for the ceremony, I don't remember a thing."

Mrs. B. finally took a break. She wiped the perspiration from her brows, drank a cup of water, and bravely continued.

"Now that I look back, I am a little easier on myself. I realize that the stupidity on my part wasn't so stupid after all. My life was out of control, and the headaches were becoming stronger and coming in closer intervals. Taking aspirin or Tylenol is what the advertisements tell you to do. Not once do they warn CAUTION: TOO MUCH TYLENOL CAN BECOME ADDICTIVE. I didn't dream that I was slowly getting hooked. Instead, I began to lose faith in the power of Tylenol altogether. Yes, I was headache free — for two hours at a stretch. Then the pain would return. I vowed to give the bottle back, to ask for a refund, and perhaps even to sue them. How could the Tylenol company cheat me like that? I was using their medication instead of others because I was afraid of getting an ulcer through aspirin use.

"I never did get an ulcer. But I did get ringing in my ears during the wedding meal. It was so loud I thought a church had moved across the street from the wedding hall. I was also nauseous and finally ate some chicken. That helped the nausea but not the ringing in my ears. It was difficult to hear people over the explosive music of the band and internal bells ringing simultaneously. Vomiting could have relieved my nausea, but nothing helped the ringing.

"I was happy when the *mitzvah tantz* drew to an end and I was able to run to visit my mother in the quiet hospital. With the corsage still on my wrist and wedding dress in tow, I rushed to her bedside, surprising the nurses who opened their mouths and forgot to close them when

I entered Mama's room. Mama was the same, critical but stable. I sighed with relief while I kicked off my shoes. Three Extra-Strength Tylenol flew out and rolled into the corner of the room.

"My head had begun to pound again. I wondered if I was getting a brain tumor. Whoever heard of someone having three headaches in one day? I promised myself that I would go to my internist first thing in the morning. Then I realized that it already was first thing in the morning. When I glanced out the window, I saw the sun was beginning to peek out of the tall building in the background, but the room was still dark. In desperation, I got on my knees and looked for my pharmaceutical treasures but couldn't find my lost Tylenol.

"I ventured to the nurse's station and kindly requested some Tylenol or some other painkiller for my headache. The nurse looked at me as if I were a UFO. 'We don't give any medication without doctor's orders,' she replied abruptly.

"I protested, 'I'm not asking for Tylenol with codeine. I realize that's a prescription drug. I'm talking about plain over-the-counter, harmless Tylenol.'

" 'Well, lady, if you like I can have you admitted, call a doctor, and then maybe give you all the medications listed in the directory. I think there are about twenty-five hundred of them.'

"I was angry and ready for a fight. 'Listen here. if I die of an aneurysm, it will be your fault.'

"The nurse wouldn't budge. 'If you had an aneurysm, you probably would be in a coma by now.'

"Suddenly I couldn't take the stress anymore. I lost all courage to fight and began to cry from exhaustion, fear, and panic. 'I just made a wedding a few hours ago. My mother is about to die, and I'm sure that I'm going to die with her.'

"The nurse finally put aside her professional stance and produced two Extra-Strength Tylenol. I grabbed them like a starving woman. I never considered that my headaches could have largely been induced by hunger. I must have looked ill, because the nurse asked no questions. She brought me a cup of hot tea and literally helped me drink it. My hands were shaking, and my body felt like the freezer at my butcher shop. The warm hot tea reminded me of a sparkling fireplace on a freezing snowy day. I whispered, 'Thank you,' as a tear fell into my cup.

"The nurse must have noticed. I will forever be grateful for her kindness. Out of nowhere she produced an apple, cereal, milk, and more tea. 'So you were saying you're coming from a wedding. Who's wedding was it anyway?'

" 'My son's,' I croaked in embarrassment.

" 'What? At Jewish weddings they don't give a dinner? I can't believe it.'

" 'They do,' I protested. 'I was just too busy to eat.' "

Mrs. B. stopped there. Our session was over. At the next session, as usual, she began talking quickly in an animated voice. At some point in our therapeutic relationship, Mrs. B. had begun to trust me. Gone was her habit of looking guiltily at the floor. Instead I found a confident woman who made direct eye contact with me.

"I did go to the doctor the very next day," she said, picking up where she had left off. He said I was suffering from tension headaches and must slow down. But I didn't slow down. I couldn't slow down. I got even busier. Three weeks after the wedding, my mother passed on to Gan Eden in her sleep. I was devastated, although not shocked. My head began pounding again the day of the funeral. By now I wouldn't dare leave the house without a drugstore in my bag. Over the next week, I consumed more Tylenol than food. When I ran out of Tylenol, I helped myself to Aleve or Excedrin. When that didn't work. I took three aspirins, which usually did the job. Instead of getting an ulcer, I got addicted to over-the-counter medication."

Mrs. B. went on, unable to control a bittersweet smile. "Can you imagine? A *frum* woman a druggie? I still can't come to terms with the shock of being labeled a drug addict, but that is what was written in my medical chart. One week after sitting shivah, I was placed flat on a bed in the hospital for four weeks. With an IV in each arm, strapped at my waist to the bedrails, bars on the window glaring at me, I became a drug-addicted patient in the detoxification ward. The screams of the other addicts and my painful horror blended well into a world of the Twilight Zone. *Baruch Hashem*, I had much support.

"For days I quivered, trembled, and alternated between being too hot and too cold. I was unable to concentrate on anything other than my shame and physical agony. I told friends and relatives not to make the three-hour drive to the rehabilitation clinic. Some came anyway, and I felt mixed emotions of relief and embarrassment. Nevertheless, their loyalty and their sacrificing an entire day to travel six hours back and forth proved how much they loved and cared about me. Their presence gave me the incentive to go on when I was depressed and had given up. Their concern made me feel loved and needed. It eased the emotional fever that soared to manic excitement only to plunge to deep depression within minutes.

"I was frightened to be so out of control, never knowing what the next minute would produce in my racing mind and body. I started to daven *shacharis* with a euphoria of gratitude to Hashem for being alive. By the time I reached the *berachos*, I was sobbing from painful depression and hopelessness. Then the letters got blurred, and I felt like a total failure, unable to do what a six-year-old can do with ease. I'd begin saying *tehillim* by heart, only to stop in the middle of a *pasuk*, forgetting the rest of the line. I felt myself going literally crazy and begged my husband to get me out of there. I was also afraid of the other patients. Some looked strange with nose rings dangling, while others rocked back and forth for hours on end. Finally, after six weeks, I was pronounced cured and allowed to go home. How I kissed the mezuzah with gratefulness and hugged my children again and again."

I told Mrs. B. how inspired I was by her courage and asked her how she felt now, two months after her discharge. I was surprised when she blurted out, "Angry. I'm so angry! How come no one ever told me about addiction to Tylenol? Maybe they were embarrassed to say anything to me when they saw me popping one pill after another. Maybe they were scared to ruffle my feathers. Maybe they didn't even notice. If only someone had stepped in. With just a little warning, I could have saved myself so much anguish. Hashem has helped me and today, I am Tylenol-, Excedrin-, Aleve-, and aspirin-free. The gory experience that came from naivete depressed me. I couldn't make peace with myself and resume the normalcy of life for which I longed. Finally, I decided that I need help putting my past where it belongs — in the past. So I came to unburden my story, and I feel much better."

In the last session, once our goodbyes were said, I plunged in and asked for written permission to write about her experience.

"If my story can prevent just one Jew from becoming addicted," she said, "then I have served my purpose in this world."

I was touched beyond words. Mrs. B. didn't believe me when I told her she was my true heroine. Her courage left me with deep inspiration.

The next time people ask, "Isn't being a social worker depressing?" I'll be prepared with my answer: "No way. I get to meet the most special people. Some of them are so strong and courageous, it makes me feel proud to have crossed their path. More often than not, I don't get depressed. I get impressed!"

Mature Adulthood

Integrity versus Despair

As individuals approach old age, they look backward, taking stock of years gone by. Have they accomplished life's goals by making the world a better place for their children? The answer leads to either satisfaction with oneself or despair that it is now too late to begin again.

The elderly are eager to give over their wisdom and what they have learned from their mistakes. Yet few children are eager to hear them, let alone heed them. Probably they, too, will falter in life, then get up and smooth their feathers. Still, they will probably not say, "I should have listened to my mother or father." Human beings learn best from their own experiences — and some don't even do that.

There is a wicked inclination in people to suppose
an old man is decayed in intellect. If a young or
middle-aged man when leaving a company does
not recollect where he laid his hat, it is nothing. If
the same inattention is discovered in an old man,
people will shrug their shoulders and say,
"His memory is gone."

— Samuel Johnson

Making the Golden Years
the Best Years

During the sunset years, priorities no longer center around personal growth. The ambitious desire to grab a handful of stars is now replaced with contentment and gratification from visits of close relatives, children, and grandchildren. The workaholic who never had time for anything begins to slow down and notices for the first time that leaves change their colors with each season. A sense of serenity fills mature adults who have led productive and active lives. Maturity enhances their appreciation for time. They use it constructively, striving to pave a better world for their grandchildren. They lend their wisdom and experiences to the younger generation, teaching them the priorities of life.

Children who are receptive gain immensely from the experiences of their parents and grandparents. They welcome the learning experience of their elders, use it to enhance their present lives, and store the wise knowledge as a guiding compass to a more successful future.

Jewish families especially respect the elderly and turn to them for guidance on many issues of life. The *zeide* who once had to work can now devote most of his day to learning the wisdom of the Torah. Bubby can now sit and connect to Hashem more than ever before. Wherever she is, it is likely that a siddur or Tehillim is close by.

Change Is Anxiety-Provoking

What was once easy now becomes hard and what was once hard now becomes easy. Once upon a time, many grandparents came from Europe to America and change was a must. From learning a new language to finding a new trade, they made the transition with steadfast resilience. Today even minor changes are difficult to adapt to. A move to a better, bigger apartment is frowned upon; the rearrangement of furniture, meant as a surprise, becomes a catastrophe. Seeing grandchildren in clothes, styles, and hairdos different from theirs creates anxiety. Change may be viewed with hostility, sameness viewed with safety.

On the other hand, grandchildren relish being spoiled by the once strict grandparents. Watching grandchildren grow up is a lot less stressful than raising one's own children. Grandparents have mellowed in their rigid expectations of children and encourage fun, playtime, and quiet talks. Often grandchildren get more compassion and material satisfaction than their parents ever did from the very same set of adults. The pressures of parenting once lay heavily on their shoulders, making child-raising a difficult and serious business. Now they can lean back and relax with the quirks, fun, and thrill of having grandchildren.

Depression

Depression can creep up at any stage of life. But if one has escaped its powerful emotional pull until now, it is not un-likely for the dragon to raise its head during this stage of life. During early- and mid-adult life, a person is too busy to deal with issues of the past. Consciously or subconsciously they put a lid on unresolved pain, such as the Holocaust, losses of loved ones, or childhood traumas. This was an absolute neces-sity in order to function as parents. Now that things have slowed down a bit, old memories begin to emerge, demanding attention, understanding, and resolution.

Unfortunately, there are few answers and many ques-tions. When logic and emotion wage war on old, buried is-sues, depression often sets in. At times the person may not even associate the depression to unresolved issues of the past. If he does, it is unlikely that he will talk about them, and for good reason. When a fifty-year-old grandmother suddenly starts to speak about a baby she lost at childbirth twenty-five years ago, people raise their eyebrows, wondering, *Is she crazy or something? Now she is beginning to agonize over the lost infant?*

Quickly the mid-life adult learns to keep secrets securely locked. No one understands or can help anyway. These up-rooted emotions once again have to return to the recesses of the mind, but they no longer have a place there. Once opened, it is hard to put the lid back on. Fears of the past invade, taking over the secure feeling of the present. Like an emotional can-cer, it spreads through the mind, slowly permeating every mo-ment of the day. At this time, two things are likely to happen. Either the depression takes its course and recedes, or it takes on momentum and becomes serious.

An indication of the latter is when physical symptoms appear. Lethargy, loss of ability to experience pleasure, crying spells, drastic change in eating or sleeping patterns, and sud-den panic attacks may indicate the need for professional intervention. It is likely that medication becomes a must to prevent nervous breakdowns, clinical depression, or suicide. Extended friends and family members must be alert and educated in recognizing the problem, seeking help, and providing support during this time.

One of the main reasons people do not get well or slip into the secondary stage of delusions and psychosis is the taboo of taking anti-anxiety or antidepression medication. The Orthodox culture frowns on such things. They carry the old European mentality, which puts all mood-altering drugs together. There is no distinction between antidepressant or psychotic medications, classifying all people who take them as crazy. But the fact is that not taking them when it is necessary can lead to craziness. Depression is *not* a disease specific to this age. It can come to anyone at any stage of life.

Dealing responsibly with depression takes more than knowledge. It takes the strength and courage to do something about it. The population must become educated and open-minded. Just as we take medication for physical ailments, at times we must take medication for negative moods. Anti-anxiety drugs serve an important purpose just the same as high blood pressure drugs. Not taking these drugs is negligence and can lead to life-threatening results. If in doubt, consult your *rav* in addition to your doctor.

Of course, when issues and fears from the past finally do come to the surface, therapy sessions where one can talk them out are a necessity. After the vital step of regaining one's balance with the proper medication, follow-up therapy is a must. No one should be embarrassed to seek help.

The Elderly

As the elderly get older, the issues that most often interfere with and challenge their contentment in life are health related. At times they must turn to their children for help, support, and involvement. They do this with mixed feelings. Logic tells them that this is part of life. One day their children will be in the same position, leaning on their own children. On the other hand, they are sensitive about their independence. Reaching out for help means losing their independence. Nothing frightens the elderly more than becoming dependent on their children due to illness or fragility.

The idea of a nursing home is taboo. Yet many elderly eventually have to submit their independence to a facility that can serve them better than their children can. Children struggle with mixed feelings of guilt, pity, shame, and relief when weighing nursing homes versus independent living. Some children can and do have their loved ones move in with them. At other times, the sick parents require care that makes such arrangements impossible. Rarely is there a perfect solution. *Rabbanim*, counselors, and doctors should all be consulted in the decision-making process. Once a decision has been made, both generations, the elderly and their children, have to accept and adjust. There are no simple answers. There is, however, faith in God, which makes every transition less traumatic for all parties involved.

It is imperative for children and grandchildren to regularly visit the home-bound relative, either at his home or in the nursing home. A visit talks. It says, "I care about you. You are an important part of my life. You are a worthwhile person. We care about you and love you." A visit from a loved one is more important than anything else. Loneliness quickly envelops the elderly like a long endless night. Visitors burst through the darkness like rays of sun, bringing the dawn of a brand-new day with promises of a better tomorrow.

Memories of one's past become more and more important as one ages. Old hurts sting less. New days are opportunities to resolve old issues. Past, present, and future unite to prepare for the World to Come. Death need not be as scary to the elderly as it is to the young. If they have lived their lives well, they have reached the highest peak of spiritual and emotional maturity. With a peace of mind we younger people cannot fully understand, they leave the future of their body, heart, and soul in the hands of God.

You Can Take Me Out of Europe, but You Can't Take Europe Out of Me!

AS A social worker in Williamsburg, I was privileged to be involved with boundless stories of *chesed* and often played an intricate part in the unfolding dramas. One typical busy day, when unexpected emergencies disrupted my tight schedule of counseling parents and children and the constant ringing of the telephone tested my patience, I vowed not to allow another disruption no matter how serious. Just as I was hanging a DO NOT DISTURB sign on my door, an elderly man poked his cane into my face. I jumped back just in time to avoid the stick's sharp point.

"You de soshel vorker, yes?" he asked in thickly accented English. The gentleman proceeded to march into my office without an invitation, much less an appointment. He took a seat before I had a chance to answer his question, and I quickly sized him up.

He was elderly, all right, probably about ninety years old. His clothes, sprinkled with ancient stains and holes, hung on his emaciated body. Evidence of poor hygiene left a lingering odor in the air. On his feet were two different shoes, one a blue loafer layered with grime and one a black lace-up shoe, also caked with dirt.

Despite his bedraggled appearance, an air of dignity hung over him. He took off his hat and matter-of-factly placed it on the middle of my desk, overlooking the empty chair beside him. I was both shocked and awed at his eccentric chutzpah but couldn't get myself to send him on his way. He was, after all, about five decades older than I and sitting comfortably in my office as if a hot glass of tea would soon follow.

"Reb Yid, what can I do for you?" I said in Yiddish.

"Ah, so you speak Yiddish? That's a surprise. You look too modern to be one of ours."

Again I repeated, "Reb Yid, what can I do for you?"

The elderly man shook his head and replied, "Notting. I don't need anyting. I'm just following de doctor's orders. He said I have to see de soshel vorker before I could go home and here I am. Maybe you need someting? A little money, a little advice? Vatever it is, go ahead and ask me. I love to help people. It's my job to help people, and I must not disappoint the holy God who gave me this job."

"I don't need anything," I said in surprise, wondering how this tattered old man could help anyone.

"Can you please tell me, den, why I have to vaste time from learning in shul to see you?" he retorted with open annoyance.

Noticing my startled face, he immediately softened his tone and tried again. "Don't feel bed. If you have a problem, just tell me. I vill try to help you. A *Yiddishe* child is a *Yiddishe* child, even if she wears makeup."

Intimidated and at a loss, I didn't dare contradict him again. I paged Dr. Rodriguez, and he immediately filled me in. The man was ninety-three years old, had no clear residential address, no phone, no source of income, no welfare, no pension, no social security, and no Medicaid. Could I please interview him and possibly assist him in getting some services and perhaps a home attendant to help him with his housekeeping and hygiene?

I sucked in my breath, said a verse from Tehillim, and began the interview. "What is your name and where do you live, Reb Yid?"

"My name is Mr. Fisher, and I live in a big house on Hooper Street. During de day it is a yeshivah, and on Shabbosos it is a shul."

"Do you know its address?"

"No, I don't. I never get mail anyway. My brodder in Bnei Brak died years ago. Since den no von writes to me, so vhy do I need an address?"

I persisted. "But what is the number of the building or house where you sleep and eat?"

Impatiently he got up to leave. "I don't know vhy you are so nosy. I am fine. I have all my needs taken care of by Hashem, Who provides for me. Besides, what's a soshel vorker anyway?" He was irritated by now. "In Europe, before the war, I never heard of a soshel vorker. Only in modern America is there such a thing as a soshel vorker, and I don't even know what it is."

He reached for his hat, and I knew my time was almost up. I had to act quickly if I was to help him. At that moment, nothing was more important to me than keeping him in my office. Mr. Fisher reminded me of someone who had just stepped off the boat at Ellis Island. Fifty-odd years of living in America hadn't made a dent in his European lifestyle, and I wondered how he survived without a home or income. By now I was so curious and impressed with his obsolete simplicity that I pleaded with him to stay so I could make his life a little more civilized. Again he insisted, even more angrily than before, that there wasn't a thing missing from his life and that if I didn't need him he was too busy to waste time from learning Torah.

Suddenly I caught on and lied through my teeth, secretly begging Hashem to understand and forgive me. "Yes, I need help, a lot of help. Maybe you could help me."

Instantly a huge smile wiped away his irritation, and he relaxed, once again placing his old hat in the middle of my desk. The phone rang and I ignored it. Someone knocked on my door and I called out, "I'm sorry, but I'm in an emergency session." The fire alarm rang, and I decided it must be a false alarm. I turned my attention to Mr. Fisher, who, with glittering eyes and raised brows, was waiting with anticipation. He sat tall and ready to serve the Holy One.

I said, "My uncle Berel lives alone, too, but he is depressed and lonely. Maybe you could help me help him. He is so poor he doesn't even have money for grape juice on Shabbos."

The old man's eyes filled tears. I felt terribly guilty and was afraid I had gone too far, but Mr. Fisher quickly composed himself and looked at me with undeserved respect. "So you are a *chesed* lady for Bikur Cholim who helps people. Vhy didn't you just tell me that right avay? Vhy such

a fancy name like soshel vorker?" Not bothering to listen
to a reply, he continued, "Okay, I vill tell you how to help
people. Tell your poor uncle to daven with a minyan
three times a day and to give a lot of *tzedakah*. That's it.
You do that, and Hashem gives you everything, even a
job like mine."

"A job?" I gasped. "But how can you work? You
shouldn't work. You should be receiving social security,
food stamps, and a pension. It's coming to you. Why
don't you take it?"

His face turned ashen, and I was afraid I might have
hurt his pride. Mr. Fisher gave a deep sigh and tried to set
me straight. "I don't need Uncle Sam to provide for me. I
have Hashem to do that for me. Besides, Uncle Sam
makes you fill out a million papers in English. Not von is
written in Yiddish. After that, you have to go to some big
building and vait there until they call your name. I vasted
a whole day of learning, vaiting and vaiting for them to
call my name. No vay, dat's not a decent vay to make a
living, as I told Hashem in my prayers. I vould not vaste
my days avay from shul just to have my name called after
four hours and then to have to go to another room and
vait another four hours till they call Mr. Fisher."

By now I knew my role clearly. I was to nod at appropriate intervals but dare not disagree nor offer any new
advice, or else he would leave. I nodded in silence while
he told his story so that my uncle Berel who doesn't exist
could benefit from the gifts of the Merciful God.

"One must never be choosy. He must take the gifts
God gives him. Yesterday somevone knocks at my door
and gives me my new hat. It is a *chassidishe* hat, so I become *chassidish* until someone gives me a newer hat. If it

is a velvet hat, I become an instant Satmarer. A few months ago I got a tall *shtreimel*. Right away I became a Gerrer. But," he continued, raising his voice and hand in great animation, "I am still a proud Satmarer with my velvet hat on weekends. Den, ven I got this hat yesterday, I became a Lubavitcher for the week."

He paused to catch his breath, and I sensed he needed some feedback to check if his time was being well spent. I quickly added that if he still had the velvet Satmar hat and wasn't using it anymore, I was certain my uncle would benefit from it. He glowed with happiness and assured me that nothing would make him happier than giving away his extra hat.

Seeing him in a good mood, I took advantage and prodded him with questions about his living conditions. I sighed with relief when he cooperated. He explained the setup. He lived in a small supply room that had a bed and bookcase in it. It even boasted a three-legged table that stood securely when supported by a pipe almost the same size as the three legs. Mr. Fisher beamed with such innocent thankfulness that I found myself being pulled into his simple and uncomplicated world. My cheeks reddened with guilt at the thought of my newly reupholstered dining-room set. Mr. Fisher immediately sensed my discomfort and assured me not to worry that his table was lopsided because just last week one of the *talmidim* from the yeshivah bought him a piece of wood to put under the pipe and now all the legs were exactly the same size.

For food he was well taken care of by the *yeshivah bachurim*, who brought him fresh milk and two slices of buttered bread every morning. At lunchtime, he was usually in the *beis midrash* learning, and he received a bowl of hot soup. As for supper, he refused to eat in the dining room with the *bachurim*. He ate the second slice of buttered bread he had saved from the morning in his room. He savored a cup of hot tea he made himself with an electric kettle that boiled water in a cup within minutes.

"But what about Shabbos?" I asked, intrigued to know how else Hashem spun miracles for him. A current of shame reeked across his face, and I knew I had pushed a sensitive button. He forced himself to reveal the secret that he worked on Shabbos and that is how he had money for all the extras, such as a bus ride, a newspaper, and Sanka coffee. I felt his humiliation and immediately regretted asking the question. Quickly I rambled that I didn't really need to know how he ate on Shabbos because my uncle Berel lived in a basement and rent included eating with the landlord and his family on Shabbos. I assured him that there was no need for him to reveal himself unnecessarily.

Mr. Fisher was confused and clearly uncomfortable. Beads of sweat intensified the odor emanating from him, and by now I was exhausted and ready to dismiss Mr. Fisher. But he seemed locked in his seat, both resenting me and yet wanting to unload his secret. Mr. Fisher announced that he wanted to take part in making a livelihood even though it was done on Shabbos because it was a mitzvah to help another Jew earn a living.

His face once again regained its dignity as he confided in an emotional whisper, afraid someone on the other side of the door might hear, "This is my wedding suit. I got married in it in 1946 immediately after the war." He beamed with innocent excitement as he related that the suit was the only remnant of the old country left to him besides his tefillin. He wore it, he said, only on Shabbos and on special occasions like today when he was visiting a doctor. "One must give respect to God's messengers," he told me.

I still didn't know what his Shabbos job was and wondered why he had changed topics so abruptly, but I didn't dare speak. It dawned on me that since it was his Shabbos suit he had to explain why he was wearing it during the week. Mr. Fisher wasn't finished and continued with the tale.

"Anyvay, as I was saying, this is how I got my Shabbos job. One day, Mr. Grossman from across the street didn't let me go home to my room after the Friday night davening. He insisted dat I join him and his family for the Shabbos meal. Of course I refused to go. I always refuse. I know that an extra mouth to feed costs money and money doesn't grow on trees, not even in America. Usually, I would buy a bottle of wine and mix it with water, and this way it would last me for three months instead of six weeks. Then I would buy two rolls for thirty-five cents each and eat it with jarred gefilte fish that lasts me four veeks. Eight pieces of fish, one for Friday night one for Shabbos lunch, and I was a rich man, with food, wine, and Shabbos spirit.

"Vell, this Friday, Mr. Grossman didn't care that I already had everything prepared for Shabbos. He begged me to come and said that their usual Shabbos guest had canceled at the last minute and now their Shabbos table would be lonely and quiet. Could I please do him a favor? I did him a favor and went to his house, but I was in for a surprise. This was no lonely couple sitting alone. Eleven children surrounded the dining-room table. If I had known, I vould never have come. I thought I was doing him a favor by livening up his Shabbos meal, but now I knew that I came for nothing. Even vorse, he talked me into coming because he felt sorry for me. This I couldn't take and refused to eat until Mrs. Grossman said that if I didn't eat she vouldn't either. Den the children said if Mommy didn't eat, they vouldn't eat either. I didn't vant to create a hunger strike, and so I ate."

I tried to maintain a straight face, but it wasn't easy. Gurgles of laughter threatened to erupt, so I looked at my nails and bit my lip. The last thing I wanted to do was laugh and possibly hurt Mr. Fisher's feelings. Quickly I changed the subject to help maintain control.

"Mr. Fisher, maybe I could send you a lady from the city to help you keep house. She would clean your room, maybe do your laundry and shop for your gefilte fish."

The wrinkles on Mr. Fisher's face suddenly multiplied as he rolled with laughter. Then he coughed and struggled to speak. I rose and gave him a drink of water. Finally, Mr. Fisher blurted out, "Now I know vat a soshel vorker is. You are a *shadchan!*" With that we both laughed. "No vonder," he continued, "you ask so many questions about me. Now I understand. No, no, and no again," he said with great emphasis. "I do not want to get married. I am too old. I can't support a vife anymore, and no decent lady vould vant an old man like me. And...my vife, may she rest in peace, vould turn in her grave if someone else took her place. No, no..."

I interrupted, "You are right, Mr. Fisher. But how about a lady from Uncle Sam to come clean, shop, and then go home? It's free from the city," I said quickly, not wanting to be misunderstood again. "Everyone has one, even my uncle Berel."

"No outside vorkers!" Mr. Fisher barked. "They steal you blind, and they even get paid for it. No, no, I could never sit down calmly with a Gemara with some lady snooping around. No vonder your uncle Berel needs help. He has a cleaner who steals him blind, and before you know it there von't be a thing left in the house for you to have as a *yerushah* (inheritance). You'd better get rid of her immediately and hope there is still something left in the house."

I reassured him that I was not going to send him a woman to marry nor a cleaner. Relieved, he got up once again to leave and blessed me to have at least twelve children so that I could duplicate the twelve tribes.

"But wait," I begged, not worrying about his pride anymore, "you never finished your story about your Shabbos job. You said you would tell me, and I'm looking for a job for Uncle Berel, too. I need your help and advice."

I knew I had said the right thing, because once again Mr. Fisher sat down smiling. "Yes, yes, I will finish my story with the Grossmans. I decided never to disturb their Shabbos again or take food from their table. They had eleven children to feed, and I didn't want to be a burden, but you vould never guess what happened." The smile on his wrinkled face once again creased into a million folds, reminding me of a map striped with dozens of lines, one blending into the other. His eyes lit up with dignity and pride.

"*Nu, nu,* so what happened?" I urged him.

Mr. Fisher was in no hurry to satisfy my curiosity. He waved his right hand in dismissal and demanded, "Don't rush me, soshel vorker. I'm a storyteller, and I tell a story my vay. If you don't like it, you can just leave."

The phone rang again, and automatically I raised my

hand but stopped in midair as Mr. Fisher's voice boomed, "Vhere is your respect, soshel vorker? I'm in middle of my story and you interrupt me?"

Suddenly feeling very small next to this elderly man, I apologized and left the phone alone.

"So, as I vas saying, I met Mr. Grossman in shul a few days later. He runs to me and shakes my hand wit excitement. 'Tank you, tank you, you don't know vat a favor you did for me and my family. This veek my business tripled in profits. Instead of making five hundred dollars profit, I made fifteen hundred dollars.' Mr. Grossman insisted the profits came because of me. He said dat ven Yaakov vent to Lavan's house, Lavan's profits doubled because Yaakov was such a big tzaddik and brought him *mazel*. Mr. Grossman insisted dat I brought him *mazel* because he had never earned such a big profit. He begged me to come again for supper Friday night and even on Shabbos for lunch to help keep his profits up. I couldn't say no to helping a man with eleven children make a living, could I? So I continued to go, and Mr. Grossman continued to make more and more money.

"One day he tells me dat he must share a little bit of the profit with me or else he vould feel guilty because it was me dat pushed his profits up. He said he vants to give me ten dollars a veek salary. I tell him dat it is too much, but he says it is too little, so we compromise and stayed with ten dollars salary every veek. I tell you, soshel vorker, I am a rich man. Sometimes, even after I buy the Yiddish newspaper, I still have some money left over so I give *tzedakah* Friday ven I go to the mikveh." Suddenly he lifted his voice and gestured, "If you need the money for your uncle Berel, I can —"

"No, no," I interrupt him, "my uncle Berel doesn't need money. He needs a job. Maybe you know Mr. Grossman's telephone number so I can call him up? Maybe my uncle can also get a job with him."

Mr. Fisher felt proud to be able to help. I noticed how little it took to make him feel important. He took out a pair of glasses that looked as ancient as his suit and opened a small calendar notebook from the year 1972. I felt awed by this elderly man who had probably gotten his glasses about the same time as the calendar book, and they both served him fine. By now I knew that offering him an appointment with the optometrist for an eye checkup and new glasses would only insult his integrity like all my previous offers.

I remained quiet as he struggled to turn the pages of the 1972 calendar book he had converted into a phone book decades ago. Finally he let out a shriek of triumph. "Here it is. Hershel Grossman, 283-9884. Don't forget to give it to him and to tell Mr. Grossman that I sent him for a job."

I thanked him profusely and bade him a final good-bye. He left, muttering a blessing over his shoulder with a sincere prayer. "Ven you get old, may you be as rich as me." The odor of mothballs tinged with foul hygiene lingered for the rest of the day, but I no longer minded.

The next day wasn't much less hectic than the day before, but I was determined to call the Grossmans at all costs. It was 11:30 A.M. when I finally found the chance. Mrs. Grossman picked up on the first ring, and I quickly introduced myself, explaining my encounter with Mr. Fisher. "Oh yes," she recalled immediately, "Mr. Fisher is our Shabbos guest."

I went on to tell her how impressed I was with their hospitality and how fortunate it was that God immediately repaid them by tripling their profits. There was sudden silence on the phone, and I thought she had hung up. "Hello, hello? Are you still there?"

She must have regained her composure because she finally whispered, "No, no, we don't own a business. My husband actually works in a garage. He fixes cars for his boss, and when business is slow and there are no cars to fix, he pumps gas at the station across the street." I was speechless, and my words locked in my throat. "Look, there must be some misunderstanding, but what difference does it make? Isn't everyone in business with Hashem one way or the other? Isn't the business between man and Hashem the best business one can have? It never goes bankrupt, and you will always have success, no?"

"Yes, yes," I finally croaked, regaining minimal power of speech. "The business between man and God is indeed the best business one can have. How lucky you are to be in such a holy business. Do you think you have room for another customer? My uncle Berel?"

"Of course, of course, just send him over. It is our privilege."

I thanked her profusely and didn't remember until hours later that I had no Uncle Berel. I only wished I did. And if not an Uncle Berel, I decided, I would even settle for an uncle like Mr. Fisher. His simplicity and pure faith had taught me more about life than all my sophisticated degrees put together.

Epilogue

We do our best to be the best parents to our children, from infant to adulthood. We strive to live life to its fullest, to be productive and giving people to our spouse, friends, and children. But there is still one more thing left to do. Let us call out to Hashem and ask Him to guide us in raising healthy children, the generations of tomorrow, and to successfully pass through every stage in life. With tefillah on our lips and bitachon in our hearts, Hashem will surely spread a bounty of knowledge over us and grant us all success.

Bibliography

Camerson-Rychlak. *Psychopathology*. Boston: Houghton Mifflin Company, 1966.

Elkind, David. *All Grown Up and No Place to Go*. New York: Addison-Wesley Publishing Company, 1984.

Goldstein. *Ego Psychology and Social Work Practice*. New York: Collier Macmillan, Inc., 1984.

Harvey, Joan C., and Cynthia Katz, *If I'm So Successful Why Do I Feel Like a Fake?*. New York: St. Martin's Press, 1981.

Hasset, James, and Kathleen M. White. *Psychology in Perspective*. New York: Harper & Row Publishing, 1989.

Thorpe, Louis P. *Child Psychology and Development*. New York: The Ronald Press Co., 1955.

Turecki, Stanley, and Leslie Lonner. *The Difficult Child*. New York: Bantam Books, 1989.

Zander, James W. Vander, and Alfred A. Knopf. *Human Development*. New York: 1978.